W9-BHM-924

THE DILEMMA
OF PSYCHOLOGY

ALSO BY LAWRENCE LESHAN

LAWRENCE LESHAN, PH.D.

THE DILEMMA
OF PSYCHOLOGY

A Psychologist Looks

at His Troubled Profession

A DUTTON BOOK

DUTTON

Published by the Penguin Group
Penguin Books USA Inc., 375 Hudson Street,
New York, New York, 10014, U.S.A.
Penguin Books Ltd, 27 Wrights Lane,
London W8 5TZ, England
Penguin Books Australia Ltd, Ringwood,
Victoria, Australia
Penguin Books Canada Ltd, 2801 John Street,
Markham, Ontario, Canada L3R 1B4
Penguin Books (N.Z.) Ltd, 182–190 Wairau Road,
Auckland 10, New Zealand

Penguin Books Ltd, Registered Offices:
Harmondsworth, Middlesex, England

First published by Dutton, an imprint of New American Library,
a division of Penguin Books USA Inc.
Distributed in Canada by McLelland & Stewart Inc.

First printing, November, 1990
1 3 5 7 9 10 8 6 4 2

Library of Congress Cataloging-in-Publication Data
LeShan, Lawrence L., 1920–
The dilemma of psychology: a psychologist looks at his troubled
profession / Lawrence LeShan.
p. cm.
ISBN 0-525-24928-1
1. Psychology—Philosophy.   2. Psychology—Practice.   I. Title.
BF38.L42   1990
150'.1—dc20   90-33192
                                                        CIP

Printed in the United States of America
Set in Goudy Old Style

Designed by Steven N. Stathakis

For Eda LeShan, who always encouraged and supported my deep love for the discipline of psychology and whose contributions to this book are too many to enumerate.

I have a lifelong debt to my teachers who taught me to appreciate the proud and clean beauty of science, in particular to Richard Henneman and Arthur Jenness. This work would not have been possible without the generosity of the Fordham Library at Lincoln Center and its head, Clement J. Ansal, who gave me permission to use their excellent resources. And, for her meaningful and practical encouragement of my work, I am deeply grateful to Mary Lawrence.

CONTENTS

Preface

LAST TRAIN FROM ARMAGEDDON

We human beings are today faced with three crucial problems. Failure to solve any one of them will certainly destroy our civilization and very probably eradicate our species. They are

- how to stop killing each other
- how to stop poisoning our only planet
- how to limit our population growth

All three involve problems, and are problems, of human behavior, thought and motivation.

We are a "scientific" society in that we look to scientists for solutions to major problems. We do not, for example, look to religion for answers, as did the population in the Middle Ages. (There when plague struck, the first—and pretty much only—line of defense was prayer.) Nor do we—as did yet older societies—seek to appease the Fates with sacrifices or scapegoats to solve our problems. We do not believe philosophy will solve major problems. We have given up hope that a change in our political structure will bring about changes on the level needed to solve them. When we become concerned about a problem we turn to science. When we become worried about a specific disease, for example, we increase the appropriations for scientific research and make it plain to the drug companies that the first one of them that comes up with a vaccine or an antidote in its laboratories will make a great deal of money.

Science has become our tool for solving important problems. For better or worse, that is *our* way. A large number of sciences have grown up, each devoted to the study of a particular realm of experience, a particular segment of reality and the solutions to problems in that area.

In the science devoted to the study of human thought, behavior, and motivation rests our hope of solving the major problems that face us now. Because of the shape of present-day civilization, we *have no other meaningful resource.*

Psychology, the science concerned with this area, is now well over one hundred years old. It can no longer have the excuse of being a young science. It has immense and trained resources of personnel. (The American Psychological Association alone has well over 16,000 members, all of whom have advanced degrees.) It has a very large number of research and study centers. It is the logical place for our culture to seek solutions to our terrifying problems. If the problems were chemical in nature, we would certainly ask chemists, if geological, geologists. Why is it that with catastrophic problems in psychology, we do not ask psychologists?

We know how serious the problems are. We know beyond doubt that our existence as a species is very much at peril. We know that we are almost constantly at war with each other in one part of the globe or another. We know that nation after nation is building nuclear arms and delivery capabilities. We know that we cannot stop killing each other and that this killing can get completely out of hand any minute. We know that the oceans are being poisoned and that when they stop functioning an adequate supply of oxygen will no longer be available. We know that our population is rapidly approaching the point where we will all starve. We know that each of these problems makes the others worse. We know that we *must* solve these problems and have no idea as to how to do this.

Our tool for solving a problem is science. Psychology is the science that deals with human behavior and inner life. We have no other tool in this society. Psychology is the Last Train from Armageddon. Why are we not getting on it? Why are there not major psychological projects—Manhattan Projects for Human Survival, Los Alamos of the Mind? Why is psychology not seen as useful in solving problems in the areas that it studies?

Unfortunately the answer is plain enough that he who runs may read. There is a widespread belief that psychology has so lost contact with real human experience that there would be no point in asking it to solve major human problems. This is the overall viewpoint of our society about one of the most basic of our sciences. It is with deep sadness as a psychologist of over forty years experience who has worked in many aspects of the field that I must agree with this opinion.

This book is an exploration of why this is so: of what happened to this science. Where did it take the wrong turn so that it is useless when most needed? Can it be reoriented so that it might provide the solutions we desperately require?

Something did go very wrong, and in the first seven chapters of this book, I show what it was and when. The correction of the problem also lies within our grasp; the last four chapters of the book show how this can be done and how we can design a truly scientific psychology that really relates to human beings and their needs. If psychology is the last hope, it is a real hope and route for our species. This book is a map of how and where we lost the path of our science and how to regain it.

Dante's *Divine Comedy* opens with the words: "In the middle of the journey of our life I came to myself in a dark wood where the straight way was lost."

Truly psychology has lost the straight way. But as Dante found a guide already waiting, so we have had our guides but we have so far largely ignored them. Let us follow them together, to see both what we have been and what we may yet be.

THE DILEMMA
OF PSYCHOLOGY

IN A DARK WOOD

In 1984 I returned to the college from which I graduated many years ago. It was here, in 1939, that I fell in love with the discipline of psychology. Since then I have always thought of myself as a psychologist and have studied and worked at that craft. But in spite of my deep identification with, and loyalty to, my profession, I have seen more and more clearly in the past few years that something has gone terribly wrong with it. We seem caught in a morass within which we make no progress; we constantly retrace our steps, putting new labels on each part of the path as we walk again and again in our own footprints.

I had come a long way in psychology since my days at the College of William and Mary. I had obtained an M.A. from the University of Nebraska and a Ph.D. from the University of Chicago. I had worked as a personnel specialist and a clinical psychologist for the Army; in an industrial consulting organization; and in the Veterans Administration. I had taught at a university, three colleges, and a theological seminary. I had had fifteen years of personal psychotherapy and five years of supervision and been a full- or part-time psychotherapist for twenty years. I had been awarded research grants from six foundations and been chief of two long-term research projects. I had abstracted articles for *Psychological Abstracts*, written seven books, co-authored two others, co-edited another. I had published over seventy-five articles in the professional journals ranging from *The Journal of Experimental Psychology* to *The Journal of Orthopsychiatry*; from *The Journal of General Psychology* to *Psychiatry: A Journal for the Study of Interpersonal Processes*; from *The Journal of Abnormal and Social Psychology* to *The Journal of the National Cancer Institute*; from the *Journal of Nervous and Mental Disease* to *Perceptual Motor Skills.*

The books and papers I had written ranged over large parts of the field: from the design of a new type of rat maze to an innovative method of obtaining electroencephalograms from patients with severe skull damage; from different ways of perceiving time in various social class groups in America to the relationship between emotional factors and the later appearance of cancer; from the psychodynamics of individuals with very high or very low accident rates to the use of a projective technique for recovering lost memories in emotionally damaged children; from the psychological design of occupational therapy programs to the relationship between ESP scoring rates and certain Rorschach variables; and from the basic structure of scientific methodology to the use of holistic health concepts.

I had organized three international psychology symposia and attended a round dozen or so more. I had been on the board of a division of the American Psychological Association (APA) and been president of a five thousand-member psychology organization. I had presented papers at over a dozen APA national conventions and given an invited address at two others. I had lectured and given seminars in many parts of this country, in Europe, and in Israel.

In short, I had pretty much done what psychologists of my time and my generation did.

Now I returned on a sentimental journey to the college and department where I had started. From the moment I entered the building in which the Department of Psychology was located, I received a number of shocks. First, the greatly increased size of the department. The two large computer rooms took up far more physical space than the entire department had covered when I was a student there. Second, was the large glass case of equipment in the hall, labeled ANTIQUE PSYCHOLOGICAL INSTRUMENTS. USE UNKNOWN. In the case was much of the equipment I had been trained to use! I could have answered questions about the equipment and demonstrated its use as well. I saw the pursuit meters we used to study motor learning, the two-hand coordination instruments, a device to study depth perception, the setup for smoking and shellacking kymograph paper, and so on. If they were "antiques," what was I?

I had an appointment later in the day with one of the professors, an old friend of mine. While waiting for the agreed-upon time, I wandered around the department, visited the psychology reading room, sat in on a couple of classes, and generally tried to get a sense of what the department was doing and what it was trying to do.

In the reading room were the latest journals of experimental and general psychology and a folder of the publications of the members of the staff. Following William James's adage that if you want to know what a science is all about, you do not ask for definitions, but instead observe what the scientists of that field are doing, I looked through them. They seemed to be mostly experimental and statistical studies of essentially unimportant aspects of human behavior. I could not help but recall the statement of James that it was no accident that experimental psychology originated in Germany. "It could only," he said, "originate in a country whose inhabitants were incapable of being bored!"

Later that day I sat in the office of my friend in the department, Ray Harcum. Two walls of the office were covered from floor to ceiling with textbooks, from introductory to advanced, in psychology. I asked him why, after over one hundred years of psychology, if one wanted *real* knowledge of human behavior and consciousness, one would not go to any of these books. Why was it, I asked him, if I wanted to know something about the *important* things of what it meant to be human—about the human condition, about love, hate, courage, jealousy, awe, dignity, terror, compassion—I would not go to these psychology texts, but to Dostoevsky, Goethe, Schubert, Picasso, Strindberg, Shakespeare? Why did *King Lear* and *War and Peace* contain and teach more psychology than all the texts on the walls? What had gone wrong with our field that this was so? Where did we make the wrong turn? I asked these questions, and then we two—both experienced psychologists who between us had worked in and studied just about every aspect of our field—looked helplessly at each other.

The question we considered with such sad and perplexed feelings was not new. We were certainly not the first to puzzle over it. Years before, the philosopher Morris Raphael Cohen had written:

> In practice, the statesman, the businessman, and even the physician may often find the suggestive remark of a novelist like Balzac of greater help than long chapters from the most scientific psychology.[1]

And, among many others, Kurt Lewin, one of our leading and most serious psychologists, put it:

> The most complete and concrete descriptions of situations are those which writers such as Doestoeveski have given us. These descriptions have attained what the statistical descriptions have most notably lacked, namely a picture that shows in a definite way how the different facts in an individual's environment are related to each other and to the individual himself. The whole situation is presented with its specific structure.[2]

Not only have we made very little progress—as British historian Arnold Toynbee put it, "We have more knowledge than our ancestors, but not more understanding"[3]—but as a profession we have lost much of our optimism, much of our hope that we ever will. The profession of psychology started out as a great dream of bringing the scientific method to bear on human beings and thus helping to develop ourselves and our species closer to the potential we all dimly perceive. The first book ever published with the term *Psychology* in the title illustrates this well. The full title was *Psychology: Thesis on the Perfection of Man*. In a real sense our slogan was the verse from the *Rubáyat*:

> *Oh love, could you and I with Him conspire*
> *To grasp this sorry state of things entire,*
> *Would we not shatter it to bits and then,*
> *Remold it nearer to our heart's desire?*

On many research fronts—sensation, perception, motivation, child development, group behavior, emotion, memory, criminology, and many others—we would probe deeper, learn more, find out how to become better ourselves and help others to become better and more full and profound human beings. We were part of a rich and glorious crusade.

I have never forgotten an incident that happened when I was a senior at William and Mary in 1941. One of the great psychologists of the time—Clark Hull—had come to visit the restoration at Historic Williamsburg, and while he was there, he consented to speak to the College of William and Mary Psychology Club. He told us that there was one thing that every psychologist should hear once in his or her lifetime, because it was the deep truth that underlay all our work, but that generally we did not talk about it or even think about it very much. He said that this concerned what a psychologist really is. "A psychologist," he said, "is a person who is trying to make a new Renaissance." This new Renaissance, said Hull, would produce a new type of individual—one who gloried in his own individuality and in the individuality of others; who could live fully and with joy in a world that science had made so small that we were all siblings whose tasks were to grow ourselves and help others grow to their fullest potential. Just as the other, past renaissances had produced new types of individuals, so would the new one. The task of the psychologist, continued Hull, is to make a difference; to increase the joy, zest, the rich-ness of life of his fellow human beings. "We psychologists," said Hull, work in different ways to bring this about: some in recruiting and training, some in theoretical development, some in research-testing the new theories; some in practical applica-tion of what is already learned. As can well be imagined, a statement like this, including the words "We psychologists," from one of the leading psychologists of the time, made to college students, made an indelible impression on many of us.

It also illustrated the hope, purpose, and optimism of that time in psychology. The high point of this optimism was shortly after World War II when our rapidly expanding ranks, our entry into and research in many new fields, and our apparent rapid progress made us feel that we were on a great crusade and had set off for a new Jerusalem.

In the following years, however, our hopes and optimism have begun to fade. We had hoped to change life on this planet: we began to despair as all our efforts appeared to have little effect. There are more psychologists than ever before, working in all sorts of jobs, but we can observe no real improvements. The thousands of psychotherapists seem to have had little or no effect on the mental health of the country. Industrial psychol-ogists do not seem to improve industry; school psychologists have had no apparent positive influence on education.

Further, the very nature of our profession seemed to be changing. We started off as a service profession. Now more and more of our colleagues appear to be viewing it largely as a busi-ness—and one that can yield a very good income indeed. It is not only that research grants have proliferated and that we all seem to be running after them. The greatest number of our new recruits are going into clinical psychology, and most of them seem more concerned about their income level than about the mental health level of their clients. Issues of the newsletters of our state psychological organizations sometimes devote more than 50 percent of the paragraphs to financial matters.

Recently a colleague handed me her card. After her name was written "Psychotherapy Associates, P.C." Guessing that "P.C." stood for some new professional degree, I asked about it and was laughed at as probably the last living psychologist to learn that this meant "private corporation." It is a method of organizing your business, I found out on further inquiry, that is only used when the income from the business is quite large. The orientation of our profession has been shifting from that of joyous crusaders to that of skeptical businessmen.

The *Psychological Monitor*, the official newsletter of the American Psychological Association, recently reported the following story:

> A newly licensed psychologist was looking for a novel way to advertise her new private practice. Her answer: a full-page ad in the local paper announcing an open house with "Psycho, the Crazy Clown," free balloons printed with her address and phone number, a "first session free" coupon, and a door prize of 20 free sessions.

Later in the same article, the *Monitor* went on to report:

> A busload of children kidnapped by terrorists were released at a shopping center, where their parents had gathered to meet them. A psychologist was there, too, passing out business cards that identified him as an expert on hostages. His material warned: "It is a well-known fact that hostages can suffer serious emotional delayed reactions. Preventive psychotherapy for your child is a must."[4]

The basic attitude these two psychologists have toward their field is too plain to require further discussion.

Although the *Psychological Monitor* raised serious ethical

questions about the above-mentioned two incidents, its own viewpoint may well be illustrated by an advertisement that it accepted and published. This is reproduced in full below.[5]

Overflow **Your Private Practice**

- Bring "dieting failures" into your office *in groups.*

- Have them *stay* for a ten-week instructional program.

- Have those in need stay for further therapy.

- Create a waiting list and fill in seasonal dips.

A unique program intended to bring *security* to the financial life of your private practice. For full information, please fill-in and mail the slip below.

Please Mail Me More Information

Name _____

Address _____

City/State/Zip _____

Mail to:

Counseling Consulting
244 Main Street
Chatham, NJ 07928

As is clear from reading it, the ad contains not a single word about the potential value of this method for the patients. There is no mention of the therapeutic validity of the program. It is *only* concerned with its value for the "financial life of your private practice." If the official newsletter of the professional organization of psychology accepts and prints advertisements such as this, what can we conclude about the value system of the organization?

During the time this chapter was being written, I spoke to a psychiatrist who told me that he was seeing patients for sixty hours a week. When I asked in astonishment why he was doing this, he replied that he wanted to buy a new apartment. I then asked if he thought that he could really do a decent job each hour and give each patient the full benefit of his experience and training; if he had the energy and capacity to help his patients with such a schedule. He looked at me, shook his head in apparent puzzlement at my question, and walked away.

The yearly national conventions of the American Psychological Association had been, in the past, vital and exciting meetings. They were filled with strong feelings, biting intellectual exchanges, long and emotional discussions in the halls, restaurants and bars of the hotel where the meeting was held. There was a deep belief in the importance and validity of our work. Most of the people there seemed to have succeeded in Robert Frost's goal in life, "To make my avocation my vocation."

More recently this has changed. The excitement is largely gone. There is much less professional talk and argument in the halls and restaurants. A muted and depressed air hangs over the meetings. The passion that once characterized these conventions seems no longer to be present. It could be a real estate convention rather than a gathering of those who saw themselves as the cutting edge of the future. Even the post of President of the Association, the highest honor that psychologists can give to one of their own, has changed. No longer does it always go to the members who are outstanding in theory and research, the spearheads of the field. More and more in recent years it has gone instead to members who have served long and faithfully on committees—the "organization men" of psychology. Since the president is elected by the total membership, this reflects a deep change in the attitudes of psychologists toward themselves.

In this book, I will analyze *where* we went wrong so that after the one hundred years of dedicated work, our progress has been minimal, our journals boring and largely useless, our hopes flagging, our ideals collapsing, and our energy levels dropping while our numbers and incomes increase. Further, I plan to show that the problem can be solved; that if we see our basic theoretical error clearly we can correct it and establish a growing, fruitful, useful, and *exciting* human science.

2

CHARTING THE
WRONG TURN

Psychologists, by and large, are as much concerned with who they are and where they are going as are the members of any other profession. Their identity crises are as frequent and severe as are those of novelists or atomic physicists. In the early 1950s, their professional organization, the American Psychological Association, hired its leading theoretician, Sigmund Koch, to undertake an intensive, long-term study of the state of the field. Where *was* psychology today? What was it doing and what had it accomplished? The study is now compiled in six heavy volumes. Koch sums us up in a sad and brutal paragraph:

> Though a massive hundred years' effort to erect a discipline given to the positive study of man has here and there turned up a germane fact or thrown off a spark of insight, these "victories" have had an adventitious relationship to the programs believed to inspire them, and their sum-total over time is overwhelmingly counterbalanced by the harvest of pseudoknowledge that has by now been reaped.[1]

Koch does not stand alone in this depressing estimate. Writing in the house organ of the American Psychological Association a few brief years ago, one of our most outstanding and productive psychologists, D. O. Hebb put it:

> It is to the literary world, not to psychological science, that you go to learn how to live with people, how to make love, how not to make enemies; to find out what grief does to people, or the stoicism that is possible in the endurance of pain, or how if you're lucky you may die with dignity; to see how corrosive the effects of jealousy can be, or how power corrupts or does not corrupt. For such knowledge and such understanding of the human species, don't look in my *Textbook of Psychology* . . . try *Lear*, and *Othello*, and *Hamlet*. As a supplement to William James read *Henry James*, and Jane Austen and Mark Twain. These people are telling us things that are not on science's program.[2]

It would be easy to present additional examples and quotations to the same effect. As early as the 1890s Wilhelm Dilthey, the psychiatrist-philosopher, wrote: "We are tired of hearing that there is more psychology in *Macbeth* than in all the psychology textbooks." Dilthey then proposed what to do about it; I will come to his suggested solution (from which I have learned much) in Chapters 9 and 10. From his time to the present, the same plaint has resounded. And now the official report on psychology, made by Koch after an extensive and intensive examination of us, comes to the same conclusion.

How is it that after so much dedicated work, we have produced so little? If the mountain labors for over a hundred years and still brings forth a mouse, the mountain had better start asking itself some questions.

If we look at the formative years of modern psychology, at the late nineteenth century when the new profession was born and had its early years of development, we can see almost at once what the great influences on its character and personality were. Psychology developed in a family and a culture, and these shaped, for better and for worse, how it grew and what it became. (It is, as if in the present we are trying to do some extensive psychotherapy because of personality faults arising from these early days. After all, if anyone knows how profound and long-lasting are the effects of early influences on later perception and behavior, it is a member of the psychological profession.)

The family in which psychology developed was the university setting. Psychology was certainly a very junior member. By the late nineteenth century, the other disciplines were grown up with status and accomplishments of their own, while psychology had yet to win its spurs. Further, all the others had rooms of their own—separate departments with their own chairmen (as high as one might go as regards prestige, power, and pay in the professional and educational side of the university). Psychology, however, was forced to room with, and remain subject to the authority of, philosophy. The psychologists were very junior and low-prestige members of the university family.

The most successful members of the university were the new, bustling, and active departments of physics and chemistry. These two elder siblings had broken away from philosophy some years before and now had the most rapidly growing departments; if new buildings were erected on university grounds, they were most likely to house these departments.

In the formative years of psychology, these departments not only held the highest status in the university, but also in the general community—the culture—as well. *Science*, meaning primarily physics and chemistry, was transforming the Western world and being written up each week in the Sunday supplements. New wonders were appearing every day and what was considered sorcery one year was commonplace and understood by schoolchildren thirty years later. The culture looked to the men in white coats, to the laboratories, to solve all the ills of the human condition and to save us from poverty, hunger, backbreaking toil, cold, and darkness. In the words of Henry

Adams, at the turn of the century, the cult of the dynamo had replaced the cult of the Virgin.

Such faith in the new sciences appeared to be justified. Wherever one looked, from the railroad train to painless surgery, from the telescope and microscope to the telegraph, powers that humankind had previously only dreamed of in legend and told stories about around the evening fire now seemed to be given to us by the new scientists. The general feeling was that the seven-league boots, the wings of Daedalus and the elixir of life were going to be produced for us any day now by the laboratory men and manufactured in the new factories that they had made possible. It was a time of hope and of new prophets, and these prophets were the physicists and chemists.

To the thoughtful psychologists in the universities, who sought to define and make a new science, a science of human beings, it seemed clear that the physical scientists were on the right track. Further, it seemed to us that the most crucial things that they had, the factor that accounted for their great success and their ability to solve difficult and complex problems, was their *method*. Whereas the seventeenth century and Descartes had given them a method for work as scientists, the eighteenth century had refined and developed it, and the nineteenth century had used it fully—with the overwhelming success we saw on every hand. The method of science had been found and its correctness and validity were shown by the results it had produced. All we had to do was to take the method and apply it to the study of human beings. By following the methods of the physical sciences, we would do for human consciousness and behavior what physics had done for matter and energy. We would learn enough so that we could bring the worst parts of human behavior under control and free the human personality to go on to new and glorious heights.

It did not occur to most of us that perhaps different areas of study, different realms of experience, might need different *kinds* of science, and that the method of physics might not be applicable to the study of human behavior and human consciousness.

The fact that our field of study featured such observables as self-consciousness and purpose, which did not exist in the realm of experience studied by the physicists, should, perhaps, have given us some clues that we might need a different method of science than they did. Indeed, some students of the problem—Ernest Rénan, Dilthey, and Wilhelm Windelband—had developed the theory of a method for *La Science de la Humanité*, a method quite different from that of the physicist, *La Science de la Nature*. This was widely known and discussed in the philosophy departments (where psychology lived at the time) at the turn of the century. However, we psychologists (as well as the rest of Western society) were so impressed with the progress of the natural sciences that we paid little attention. Also, the cultures of Europe and America had come to the conclusion that anyone who used the method of the natural sciences was "hardheaded," while anyone who didn't was "softheaded." (William James said that America divided people up into "redbloods" and "mollycoddles.") The conventional wisdom was that only the hardheaded red-bloods made any progress. As participants in our culture, we psychologists believed this too. And since we wanted to make progress, which meant being hardheaded and like the physicists, we chose to follow their methods. This was done to such a degree that Sigmund Koch was able to say without exaggeration:

> The history of psychology, then, is very much a history of changing views, doctrines, images, about *what* to emulate in the natural sciences, especially physics.[3]

A method is far more than specific techniques. It involves philosophical assumptions as to how to make progress. These basic ideas are far more important than the techniques that develop from them. Techniques change with the times; the ideas behind them are far more stubborn and resistant to change. Mechanical engineers don't use slide rules much anymore (a slide rule is getting as hard to find—except in antiques stores—as an abacus); they now use pocket calculators instead, but the ideas behind the use of slide rule and calculator are the same and the reasons for using them remain the same. We in psychology could not take the specific techniques from the physical sciences—we had little use for their spectroscopes and voltmeters—but we did take the basic ideas from the method of the physical sciences and use them as the basic ideas for a science of our own. There are five of these basic concepts and, without examining them closely (indeed, rarely even verbalizing them), we built modern psychology on them. I shall state them briefly here and discuss them more fully in the chapters that follow.

I will then discuss what a scientific method designed to study human consciousness and behavior—as opposed to the current method used by psychology, designed to study inanimate objects—would be like and what it might accomplish.

The five basic concepts we took from nineteenth-century physics are

- the concept of the correct method to train specialists
- the concept of the value of the laboratory
- the concept that everything is quantitative and predictable
- the concept that you can make a metaphor of anything you are studying
- the concept that God is an engineer

These five assumptions are not very frequently verbalized in the halls of academic psychology, where the present practitioners in the field were trained and where future psychologists are now undergoing their initiation courses and rites. If the premises *are* clearly stated, we respond to many of them with, "Of course that's only partially true." Or, "That used to be true, but it's not anymore. Why do you go around flogging dead horses?" (That profound explorer of the human condition Arthur Koestler has an essay on the S.P.C.D.H.—the Society for the Prevention of Cruelty to Dead Horses—in which he shows how widely this approach is used in all scientific, political, and cul-

tural fields to keep us from facing basic issues and making progress.[4])

Whatever the response, it is only necessary to pick up half
a dozen recent psychological journals at random, or to wander
the halls of a modern university psychology department and
listen to the lectures and discussions, in order to be aware that
these assumptions not only continue to be widely accepted, but
are the pillars on which the entire field is resting. As we all
well know today, it is the unverbalized assumptions that have
the most power over us. By stating these here baldly and exploring them in the following chapters, I hope to make it less
possible to continue to accept them without careful evaluation.
Only after a pattern of behavior has been made conscious can
we decide whether or not we wish to continue it. These assumptions have not been considered consciously very much of
the time, but we have acted as if we were certain that they
were true. And they have almost completely paralyzed and
stunted the growth of one of the great hopes of humankind. In
the words of the old Yankee maxim: "It ain't what you don't
know that hurts you, it's what you know for certain that
ain't so."

3

HOW TO TRAIN SPECIALISTS

One of the great inventions of the eighteenth century was the idea that the way to greater understanding of a field was to train people to specialize in that area, focusing their study narrowly and concentrating their time and effort. As the field became more and more limited and narrow, penetration into it would become greater, and we would move into deeper and deeper understanding.

During the eighteenth and nineteenth centuries, this seemed to work. It was reflected in, and increased by, the way university departments became increasingly specialized: the Department of Natural Sciences, for example, breaking up into departments of physics, chemistry, geology, and so on almost ad infinitum. The old humorous definition of a specialist as "one who knew more and more about less and less until he knew almost everything about almost nothing" seemed every year to become closer to the truth.

This approach works to some degree in the physical and biological sciences, although its value was generally more apparent than real. It provided good training for many of those who do the detail work, who do the everyday investigations and make the small, pawnlike advances that eventually make the large, conceptual changes possible. However, this kind of training was not efficient, by and large, even in these sciences, for those who actually made the large advances, those who help their field perceive the data in new ways.

The leading figures in physics and chemistry, those who made the great strides that changed our world, the Einsteins, Plancks, and Bohrs, were Renaissance men with a wide range of interests. At the famous Copenhagen Conference of 1932, for example, in which a major view of reality in physics was worked out and in which the great names in physics of the period were present and active, there was enough musical talent and training for a first-rate orchestra. In addition there was enough dramatic talent so that a play about the conference was written as it was in progress, and read (if not acted), aloud.

And however much the narrowing and focusing technique works for specialists in other areas, it does not work at all for increasing our understanding of human beings, whose behavior and consciousness are not divisible into parts that then can be studied separately. We may have separate chapters in our textbooks that, in a tradition many hundreds of years old, discuss "thinking," "feelings," and "will" separately, but to study each of them alone is about as useful and realistic as studying the hardness of a piece of metal with no discussion of its temperature. Humans function as wholes in an interpersonal and physical environment, and they cannot be understood without recourse to an understanding of these. If that great expert on the behavior of apes, Wolfgang Köhler, could say, "A solitary chimpanzee is not a chimpanzee," how much more true is this of a human being?

Those who have helped us make the real advances in psychology have certainly known this, have known that it is the broader and broader view that brings us to an understanding of human consciousness and behavior, not the reverse. Freud was once asked who were the three greatest psychologists that ever lived. He answered that Dostoevsky was the first and Goethe the second. ("As for the third," said Freud, "modesty forbids!")

The amount of understanding and communication we can have of and with another person depends largely on how rich and broad a background we can bring to the relationship. When a patient speaks to us of his experience with murderous thoughts, our comprehension will be much more profound if we not only bring to the situation our own experience of our own murderous thoughts (and this is one reason, of course, that long and serious psychotherapy is *essential* if one wishes to be a psychotherapist—so we can bring our own experience to our work), but also have learned about this type of feeling from Iago, Clytemnestra, and Raskolnikov. If our patient speaks to us of loving, our comprehension is greater if we have learned not only from our own loving, but also from Anna Karenina, Elizabeth Barrett Browning, and the Shakespeare sonnets.

A very wide training is important if we wish to be psychologists and "meet" and "comprehend" and "communicate with" other people. The more I know of human consciousness and behavior in its widespread forms, the more likely I am to comprehend a particular "other." If I have experienced Prince Mishkin through the genius of Dostoevsky, I am more likely to *know* the experience of a particular patient who is striving to awaken himself to something he does not yet comprehend, but knows is within his potential, than if I had not read *The Idiot.* If I have been touched by Schubert's *Die Wintereise,* I am far more able to understand the sadness of another person's experience. If I have met and listened to Socrates through the love Plato had for him, I am more likely to be able to understand the New York City Ilyosha Karamazov who tells me that it is better to suffer injustice than it is to commit it.

As a seasoned telegrapher listens to the same staccato blur of sounds that I do, and, in it, because of his training and experience, meets, and does not doubt that he meets, another human being and *hears* him, so the more training and experience I have, the more likely I am to meet and hear another person through the blur of signals he sends out.

In order to organize our knowledge and be able to use it as therapists, we must also have learned Freud, Sylvano Arieti, and Carl Rogers. This is essential, but far from enough. The task of a therapist is constantly to grow himself, to expand his experience and his soul so that he can not only bring more and more to his patients, but also can say to them, "Do as I do, as well as say." We teach, in the deepest way, by example. If a therapist wants his patients to grow, he must himself constantly struggle to grow. He must understand what Meister Eckhart meant in the fourteenth century when he wrote:

> *There is no stopping place in this world, no, nor was there ever one for any man, no matter how far along his path he'd come. This above all then, be always ready for the gifts of God and always for new ones. And always remember, God is a thousand times more ready to give than you are to receive!*

To understand the *meaning* and *tone* of our patient's experience we need Shakespeare and Schubert, Picasso and Rilke. To understand the *structure* of these experiences and how the reactions to them can be modified, we need Freud and Jung, Otto Rank and Alfred Adler, Harry Stack Sullivan and Adolph Meyer, Karl Menninger, and Victor Frankl.

The psychologist William McDougal firmly believed that psychology required such resources of maturity, sensitivity, and knowledge as made it inappropriate to teach at the undergraduate level. Although many of us might not go quite so far, there is certainly something to ponder here.

The goal of training in psychology—what we really wish to teach our students—is to comprehend how character and personality develop, change, grow. How the themes and parts of an individual swell and recede and form harmonious and inharmonious patterns. How different patterns of being respond to different environmental patterns. In these areas we humans have learned much—Shakespeare knew more than Homer, and Arthur Miller knows things that Shakespeare did not. (For example, about the effect of culture on personality development.) Yet there is much more to learn, and we hope our students will continue to progress in comprehension of what it means to be a human being. To do this, however, they must concentrate on the whole person, on the richness and complexity of being human, they must take their orientation as much from Tolstoy as from B. F. Skinner.

My first control, or supervising, therapist was a widely trained and highly literate psychiatrist named Marthe Gassmann. During one session, after she had been supervising me for several months, she turned to me and said, "Well, Larry, isn't it time we started getting you educated?" I bridled at this and muttered that a Ph.D. from the University of Chicago meant *something.* She replied (and I still remember her words clearly), "Oh, yes, you know quite well most of what is important in the psychology and psychiatry textbooks. You know nomenclature and the theoretical models of Freud and Jung and how they are alike and how they differ. You know how to reflect feelings and interpret dreams. But the best of the human race, for thousands of years, have been trying to understand what it means to be human and to be in the human condition. They did not write in the textbooks. They wrote plays and stories, composed music and painted pictures. And in these things you are an ignoramus. Yes, you know and love poetry, and that is a good start. In the field of psychotherapy you are a pretty fair mechanic. You have to decide whether you want to become a better mechanic or you want to become a therapist."

I sulked for a while and then allowed that I would prefer to become a therapist. She smiled, said, "I thought you would say that," and handed me a study list. I still have it. On it are Plato's *Republic, Paradise Lost,* and some Carlyle to read; certain pictures in the Metropolitan Museum of Art in New York to look at, and some particular records to listen to. Later she gave me other study lists and presently I achieved enough understanding of what she meant and enough momentum to continue on my own.

* * *

From this experience I learned much about the meaning of Marthe Gassmann's statement. I will not refer a patient to a psychotherapist unless the therapist is at home with at least one other approach to the human condition than that contained in the professional literature. The therapist does not have to be a composer or a musician, but must comprehend and be deeply responsive to classical music; or he or she does not have to be a playwright or actor as long as there is understanding of, and response to, the great teachings of the theater. Similarly for painting, theology, and philosophy.

Although this idea has been understood and accepted by the leading figures in the clinical fields of psychology and psychiatry, by Freud, Jung, Adler, Kurt Goldstein, Andreas Angyal, and others, it has often been forgotten in our frequent backsliding. Psychiatry trains therapists who know only one approach to human beings, often one no wider than formal diagnosis and appropriate chemical medication. Social workers often know only "reflection" or psychoanalytic concepts. Psychologists may know only Transactional Analysis or "Gestalt" techniques or some other single approach. Many of these set up private practices and make money passing themselves off as psychotherapists, often having had very little training, no personal psychotherapy, no supervision by anyone but a member of their own school.

It is often, unfortunately, worse than that. I recall in the mid-1970s accidentally being seated on the bus leaving a professional meeting next to a charming woman who had a full-time psychotherapy practice and was even certified in her home state to practice. She had a master's degree, and, on questioning, admitted with no trace of embarrassment that she had never read a complete book by Freud, Rogers, Rank, Jung, Goldstein, or Adler. Or, so far as I could tell, by any others of the serious thinkers of the field. Further, she had never had any personal psychotherapy or supervision, but had been to a good number of weekend workshops at Esalen Institute and similar places. She had written a book on how to masturbate, which struck me as rather funny ("What," I asked her, "do you say after stating that a lubricant may be useful?"), but which she took seriously. If psychotherapy is in the future regarded as the greatest hoax of the twentieth century, it will be because of the people we have allowed to practice it.

And in the field of academic psychology the training is as narrow as it is in the clinical field. In academic psychology we train people in narrow, provincial, *lifeless* views of human beings, replete with statistics that further desiccate our concepts of what it means to be human. We then expect them to contribute to our understanding of the problems of living with ourselves and each other, of why we cannot stop damaging ourselves, killing each other, and poisoning our only planet. The academic psychologists, by and large, seem determined to have as little to do with real life as he or she possibly can. If they cannot substitute white rats for people, they will make a determined effort to substitute computers. One can legitimately ask what the rat and the computer are doing in the psychology laboratory—what either one has to do with the joys and pains of being human. As Arthur Koestler put it about two of the more prominent academic psychologists:

> Both [Watson and Skinner] are engaged in question-begging on an heroic scale, apparently driven by an almost fanatical urge to deny at all costs the humanity of the man and the rattiness of the rat.[1]

One major problem in changing the training of our psychologists is that the people who administer the present training are themselves the judges of how "good" and "successful" the products of their training are. They are the ones who offer teaching jobs in the universities, who give recommendations, decide on the awarding of degrees, and so forth. William James wrote in a similar context: "No priesthood ever originates its own reforms." And so we continue with an old model for training psychologists, one that is irrelevant to the real problems of human life.

The root model that is fundamental to the training of all
psychologists, regardless of the student's area of interest,
and most importantly, regardless of his particular talents
or proclivities, is simple enough to identify . . . it is the
experimental research scientist. *Students not only have*
this model as the core of their curriculum design, the judge-
ments made on them during their schooling, etc., but also
in their Ph.D. thesis. In this way they are intensively train-
ing to believe that "only conventional types of research
are worthwhile."[2]

If the training program emphasized turning out research scientists equipped and oriented to help us learn more about human
beings, to help us see deeper into the great and terrible problems we face, no one could argue too strongly with this. The
problem is, however, that today's training turns out research
scientists on the ideal model for work in the minor aspects of
the nineteenth-century physics. We graduate people who know
how to do research on things that can be seen and touched,
that can be quantified and described in numbers, that fit the
mechanical model so well illustrated by the steam engine. Since
behavior and consciousness fit none of these categories, it is
only the smallest and most trivial aspects of humanity that they
can study, but they do study these with very great precision and
in remarkable detail. Few of them seem to have heard of the
scientific maxim that Graham Bennette, director of the British
Cancer Council, used to have hanging over his desk: IF AN
EXPERIMENT IS NOT WORTH DOING, IT IS NOT WORTH DOING WELL.

William James knew well the direction academic psychology was taking and what was happening in the field. Although
he fought against it, he was too wise to deny it. When after a
great deal of demand on the part of his publishers that he con-
dense his classic two-volume work, *Principles of Psychology,* to
one volume, he agreed to do so, he wrote to his editor:

By adding some twaddle about the senses, by leaving out
all polemics and history, all bibliography and experimental

details, all metaphysical subtleties and digressions, all hu-
mor and pathos, all interest in short, and by blackening
the tops of all the paragraphs, I think I have produced a
tome of pedagogic classic which will enrich both you and
I, if not the student's mind.[3]

It is not only in this country that we have been training academic psychologists to stay away from the intensity and meaning of human life, from its *reality*, as much as possible. The
situation has been the same in England. The psychologist Liam
Hudson has described well his years in the experimental psychology departments of Oxford and Cambridge in the 1950s:

Experimental psychology in Oxford had at that time
much in common with analytic philosophy. . . . Any
explanation we offered, any theory we postulated, any
result we described had to be defined operationally—
in terms of input and output, stimulus and response.
We were set to do science in exactly the way that the
chemist or physicist does it. Our experiments, like
theirs, had to be work that any technically competent
stranger could replicate. . . . In dusty rooms, scruffy as
only experimental psychologists can make them, we
sorted cards, watched flashing lights, pressed bars, and
once or twice watched white rats wander disconso-
lately through poorly constructed mazes. We discovered nothing of much interest, either about the rats
or about ourselves; and it was never hinted that we
might. Our highest ambition was to refute a theory;
or, failing that, to lend it conditional support. Any
idea that we were there to uncover the mysteries of
the human mind, to plumb the depths of the psyche,
would have been greeted with embarrassment; the
kind of embarrassment that hardens into derision, and
eventually into contempt. Just as a man on a desert
island was held to illuminate the moral order, so a rat

or monkey or student pressing a bar was thought to illuminate the brain. . . .

Such assumptions about research were rarely discussed, and as far as I can recall, never critically examined. Sustaining them, inarticulate, were certain more pervasive beliefs about knowledge itself . . . that science is built by piling one fact upon another; a quasi-religious faith in the ideas of stimulus and response; a distrust of any but precise, small-scale theories; a contempt for social science, and disregard for any social or cultural process; an avoidance in research of personal feelings or personal experience; and a taste for mechanical and electronic metaphor. Above all, we believed in "objectivity."[4]

Hudson's descriptions will not sound strange to the average senior or graduate student in the usual psychology department of today. Indeed the question likely to be asked would be: "Why does he seem critical of these ideas? That's what psychology is all about."

That this is so and that the student is responding in terms of the way he or she has been trained to view psychology is indeed depressing. The student enrolls with hope and idealism in the first course in psychology, wanting to understand the human condition. Three years later he has learned that distinguishing between theories about the figural after-effect (a minor anomaly of the eye) or measuring the exact limits of color constancy (another minor anomaly) is the important kind of thing that psychologists do. Our ability to so change students' viewpoints in a few years is indeed marvelous. This ability is helped by the aesthetic of precise, small-scale work. I remember running rats through mazes, and the neatness and satisfaction of the columns of figures I recorded as I measured exactly the amount of time they hesitated at each choice point and correlated these times to the eventual selection of a correct or wrong choice. I felt, at the end of an afternoon of this, both very scientific and aesthetically satisfied. It did not occur to me for many years afterward that the activity was pointless and meaningless and would have no effect on human life.

I, however, was one of the lucky ones. I had a marvelous teacher—Richard Henneman—a specialist in depth and form perception, who taught us that there was no one way to look at human beings, that all systems limp and that any real understanding of what it means to be human needs a number of angles of approach. In Wittgenstein's terms, there is no one definitive photograph that we can make. We can, however, choose a landscape and develop an album of sketches that would truly illuminate the terrain.

One course that all majors in psychology were required to take was in the systems and theories of psychology. Henneman started by teaching Behaviorism as a devout Behaviorist. With zeal and fire he went through the first six weeks and at the end of it, we were all convinced and dedicated Behaviorists. He then suddenly shifted and taught the next six weeks as a completely convinced Gestaltist. Then a period of psychoanalysis, one of William Stern's Personalism, and so on. At the end of the year we *knew* that there was value and truth in all of the systems, that none had exclusive rights to the territory, and that no one theoretical model could ever encompass the wonderful and complex thing that was a human being. We had learned that the wider our view, the more theoretical viewpoints we learned, the more sketches there were in our album, the more we could bring to our work as psychologists.

Years later I came to realize that what applied to the study of academic psychology applied to psychotherapy as well: different patients were best worked with from different points of view and that there was no therapeutic approach that was useful for everyone who consulted me. During this period I attended a lecture at the Westchester Child Guidance Clinic. The speaker was a child psychiatrist named Annina Brandt, a lovely, zestful woman who must have been in her late seventies at the time. She talked of how it felt to be a child, of the long thoughts and sudden changes of mood, of the need for love and the often incomprehensible perceptions of adults' activities. The staff, which was quite orthodox psychoanalytic, became more and more uncomfortable. Finally one of them interrupted her: "Dr. Brandt, what school do you belong to?" Brandt looked quite puzzled and hesitated. Finally she replied with, "But how can I tell until I see the child?"

Since then, I have learned from my own experience that there are Freudian patients, Jungian patients, Existentialist patients, and dozens of other varieties. There are patients with whom I have been on a first-name basis at the end of the first session, where it was "Joe" and "Larry," and there are patients with whom I have been on a formal, last-name basis after three years—"Mr. Jones" and "Dr. LeShan," with a formal handshake at the beginning and end of sessions. There are patients who worked well with me, and patients who didn't. (Indeed, it is my belief that an honest psychotherapist refers to other practitioners at least a third of the patients who come to him on the basis that he is being hired to help the patient find the best for himself and the best is a different therapist with a different personality.)

I remember one patient who taught me much about individual differences. She was a lovely, vital woman with a metastasized melanoma. During the sixth session, she turned to me and asked if I really believed all the words I had been saying about individual differences and each person finding his or her own path and rhythms of life. I answered that I thought I did and she replied, "Well, then, why haven't you been listening to a word I've said?" I answered that I thought I had been, but that apparently there was something very important that I had missed and if she would spell it out for me, I would try to understand. From then on, our conversation went roughly as follows:

SHE: How often do you see a patient with the kind of problem I have?

I: Usually twice a week. Sometimes once a week for periods. Perhaps at other rare times, three times a week.

SHE: That's still pretty rigid. A real Procrustean bed. And each session is an hour, isn't it?

I: Yes.

SHE: I've told you three times during our work here how *I* learn. And you never heard me. I learn new things in "crash programs," periods of intensive work followed by periods of digestion. If you do believe what you have been saying about individual differences, then we will work in the following way: I'll see you four or five times a week for a time and then I will decide it has been enough and not see you for a month or two or three. And don't call me, I'll call you. When I'm ready we will begin to work again on another crash program. Is this okay with you, or was it just words you were giving me?

I had little choice but to agree, and I also felt the justice of her words. We worked together in this way for two and a half years, by which time she "graduated" with no further sign of her melanoma being present. Twenty years later, she is still alive and healthy, living her own individual life with zest and enjoyment.

Since then I have never decided in advance what the program and timing for a patient should be. (I have also checked and found that there is no research indicating that there is a "correct" time length for a session of psychotherapy that applied to more than one patient. The one-hour length was originally set because it was the most convenient way for the therapist to schedule appointments. Many therapists later shortened sessions to fifty minutes, because they wanted to keep the ease of scheduling and still have a ten-minute rest between appointments.* I have seen patients for periods ranging from twenty minutes at a time to two hours or more. Further, each

---

*After going to fifty minutes, some psychologists observed that what was true for the candy-bar manufacturers was true for their own profession: This was that you can diminish the quantity of your product at the same time you increase the price and still have a salable product. They therefore went to forty-five minute sessions and raised their prices. During the procedure there was no corresponding increase in the quality of the product. The next step in this sequence remains to be seen.

patient has a best *style* of using the session, a way of working that will enable him to benefit to the maximum from the interaction with the therapist. Some do best with more activity on the part of the therapist, some with less. One patient I worked with did best if I said nothing the first twenty minutes while she talked about how she felt and what had happened since the last session. Another worked far better if the first five minutes were devoted only to general matters, politics, the arts, and so on. It allowed free, interactive conversation for this period; he would then plunge strongly into the psychotherapeutic work. There were other patterns also and, I am sure, many that I was not skilled enough to observe. I try to be aware of the best pattern for each patient and follow it. Sometimes, of course, I will at one point or another, interpret a patient's particular pattern to him as an example of the way he interacts with others. Each person is different and must be worked with differently—but if I had been trained in only one approach, and if I had not had the guidance of a Dick Henneman and a Marthe Gassmann and others, I would never have noticed this.

In those fields of science where the professional works with nonhuman material, it may well be legitimate for the educational program to focus in a narrow way and concentrate study on one small facet of the field. The evidence is that this does not make for people who can make the large theoretical advances—as I noted earlier, by and large even in the physical sciences, the bigger advances were made by scientists with wide, rather than narrow, backgrounds—but the viewpoint can at least be defended.

In those fields where the professional will work with human consciousness and behavior, however, the opposite of this viewpoint is clearly true. As the great writers and artists have known, human beings are each a rich and complex tapestry of many colors and shades; they are a part of their family, of their culture, of their biological heritage. There are ways in which each one is like all other human beings, ways in which each is like the members of a culture or a smaller group, ways in which

each is like no one but himself. To see them, at least as concerns any more important activity than how quickly people
blink an eye in response to a puff of air, takes wider and wider
viewpoints on the part of the psychologist because the matter
of psychology is at all times affected by, and responding to, the
deep as well as the shallow currents of being.

Many of these currents that always affect our subjects—
again, once we start dealing with the specifically human qualities of human beings—have been studied in far greater depth
by the novelist, the composer, the poet, and the philosopher
than by the academic or the clinical professional. To turn out
psychologists with no training in the searches for the "best of
the human race," through all the millennia of which we have
records, on what it means to be a human being, is like turning
out physicists with no knowledge of mathematics.

4

THE LABORATORY
AND THE WORLD

It may be a good idea to start the discussion of the hypothesis that anything of importance in science can be discovered in a laboratory with an example of the pitfalls and dangers of studying behavior—let alone consciousness—in the laboratory.

A very great deal of psychological research has been done on the white rat. Leaving for a later chapter the reasons for this, as well as a discussion of the validity of trying to generalize from rats to people, let us simply look at one experience with studying rats in our traditional ways of psychology.

Rats have been practically ubiquitous in our laboratories and, since psychologists are both trained and interested observers, the sex lives of the rats quickly came under professional gaze. To our surprise, the sex life of the rat was quite atypical for mammals: it was essentially continuous, following no cyclic patterns; it was always initiated by the male, the female being generally unresponsive or resistant—and, to be pretty anthropomorphic about it, she often gave the impression of being bored. This phenomenon was observed over and over again, and a great many generally consistent professional papers were published about it.

Then along came the ethologists, who study animal patterns of behavior in natural conditions. They reported that in the wild, the sexual behavior of rats was very different. It followed cyclic patterns and was always initiated by the female. The way she initiated it was to come within three or four body lengths of the male.[1]

The reasons for the difference between laboratory and natural-setting behavior quickly became obvious. In a laboratory cage, it was *impossible* for the female to get more than three or four body lengths away from the male. The cages were simply too small! From the male's point of view, the female was constantly "coming on" to him and, to repeat our anthropomorphic viewpoint, from her point of view, he was a sex maniac! Behavior in the laboratory was clearly irrelevant to behavior outside of it. Because, most of our experimental work takes place in laboratories, this raises some pretty serious questions.

As biologist Sir Peter Medawar has pointed out, there is the feeling among those interested in science that there is something *essentially meritorious* about experimentation. This attitude started with Francis Bacon and has grown gradually since then. Observing your data in a natural state was, and generally is, seen as somehow unscientific. This is why an eminent neurophysiologist said of ethology, "Why, that's just birdwatching, isn't it?"

There are strong lessons here that we will have to look at in more detail. A good deal of the time, at least, our laboratories are highly artificial situations that seriously distort the behavior—and therefore our interpretations—of humans or whatever other species we are studying. Further, we shall have to question whether even the subjects we use are adequate to our goals.

That gentle and wise German psychologist, Max Wertheimer, the man who started the Gestalt revolution in our field and was the teacher of both Kurt Koffka and Wolfgang Köhler, emigrated to the United States quite late in his professional life. After he had been in this country for some time, he was asked what impressed him most about it. He replied that it was the nature of the population, that it was so varied and made up of so many different kinds of people. After reading the American psychological journals for so many years, said Wertheimer, he had become convinced that the population of this country was made up exclusively of white rats and college students.

As we psychologists ruefully grin with a half-ashamed recognition at this remark, questions come to our minds. What *are* we doing and what have we been doing in our psychology laboratories. What kind of validity do our data have? What kind of *importance* do they have?

The science of the eighteenth and nineteenth centuries made its great and dramatic advances in understanding the behavior of things that could be seen and touched. These were things to which there was "public access"—all humans who looked at them could observe them and, if they looked well, would observe the same things and occurrences. At the stage that science was in during these centuries, and studying these kinds of things, most important things *could* be discovered in a laboratory.

Due to these two factors—the kinds of things science (physics, actually) was studying and the stage that science was in—the concept gradually became established that anything of importance in science could be discovered and validated in a laboratory if one was ingenious and careful enough. As psychology developed and psychologists tried to be as "scientific" as the physicists whom they perceived to be so successful, this assumption became established as a generally unverbalized axiom of the field. Laboratory work, we assumed, is *the* way to learn about human consciousness and behavior. (However one formally defines psychology, if we are not trying to learn about one or both of these, we are not working in psychology.)

Questions have been raised about this for a long time now, but we have paid very little attention to them. The questions came most dramatically from the fields of psychiatry and clinical psychology, whose practitioners clearly believe that one can learn more about the consciousness and behavior of people in a clinical office than in a laboratory. However, this is not a real challenge, since the consulting office is simply another form of laboratory with many of the same limitations that plague our more traditional research rooms. The real challenge has come from within our own ranks, from trained and accepted research psychologists who have asked the disturbing question: Can we learn *anything* worthwhile about human consciousness and human behavior in a laboratory?[2]

Egon Brunswik, for example, has been insisting since the 1930s that individual behavior and feeling cannot be interpreted or made sense of unless we can know and describe how the person perceives and responds to the environment in which they occur. This—the "ecological validity" by means of which each experiment and observation was to be judged—was ignored. It meant that psychologists must look at their laboratories as environments *and at themselves as important entities in that environment.* Since, however, physicists and chemists do not have to look at themselves in this way, psychologists were extremely reluctant to undertake to do so.

In 1947, Gardner Murphy emphasized that behavior manifests itself in human interactions and therefore can never be deduced from isolated performances in perception, learning, and so on—or from the typical psychology laboratory situation.

Roger Barker has long insisted on what he calls "Behavior Settings" as one of the crucial elements in designing experiments. The *meaning* to the individual is an essential part of the definition of the Behavior Setting.

American philosopher and educator John Dewey, in 1899, put it in the following way:

> The great advantage of the psycho-physical laboratory is paid for by certain obvious defects. The complete control of conditions with resulting greater accuracy of determinations demands an isolation, a ruling out of the usual

media of thought and action, which leads to a certain re-
moteness and easily to a certain artificiality.[3]

This warning, delivered in Dewey's 1899 Presidential Address
to the American Psychological Association, was understated
and muted. Clear though it was, Dewey still had no idea of the
degree to which it would apply a century later. When he wrote
it there were only a half-dozen or so psychology laboratories in
the world, and the tendency to shift all psychological study into
them was barely under way. As he noted:

When the result of laboratory equipment informs us, for
example, that repetition is the chief factor influencing
[memory] recall, we must bear in mind that this result is
obtained from nonsense material—i.e., by excluding the
conditions of ordinary memory.[4]

Indeed, this is an excellent example of the fatuity of most laboratory studies. It *is* true that these experiments show that repetition is the chief factor affecting what we remember. It is true
in the sterile recesses of the laboratory, with nonsense syllables
or words paired in patternless ways. When we come to real life,
however, matters are quite otherwise. How many old women
did Raskolnikov have to murder before he would remember the
fact all his life? How many times did Keats have to read Chap-
man's Homer before it created an indelible impression on him?
And for each of us, how often does a parent have to die or a
child be born before you remember it for the rest of your days?
Most laboratory experiments have the same relationship to the
real-life occurrences of human beings as does the sexual behavior of the white rat in the laboratory cage and in the wild.

Psychiatrist Erich Fromm put the matter thusly:

Behavioral psychology may be a science, but it is not
a science of man. It is rather a science of alienated
man conducted with alienated methods by alienated
researchers. It may be capable of illuminating certain

aspects of human nature, but it does not touch on what is vital, on what is specifically human about human beings.[5]

We often forget, when conducting laboratory experiments with human subjects, that they may be having vastly different experiences than we believe they are or than the experiment has planned for them. In the words of the philosopher Alfred North Whitehead:

> That men closely coordinated in action may remain worlds apart in mental experience is the veriest commonplace. Broken partnerships in business, marriage, politics show too clearly how persons may live through the same events, engage in the same tasks, speak the same language, yet their alienation remains complete.[6]

It would be easy to multiply examples such as these. What is generally being said here is that the psychology laboratory is an artificial situation, far removed from "real life." When a subject steps into a psychology laboratory, he steps out of his culture, and all the normal rules and conventions are temporarily discarded and replaced by the single rule, "Do what the experimenter says no matter how absurd or unethical it may be."

One widely reported set of experiments that illustrate the points I am making were the Milgrim studies. In these a subject was shown another "subject" in a different room who was strapped in a chair with electrodes attached to him. The first subject was told that the other (who, unknown to him, was really another experimenter with fake, unattached electrodes) had volunteered for a "learning" experiment. He had to learn to respond correctly to cue words, and, after each wrong answer, the subject was to give him an electric shock. As more incorrect answers were given, the shocks were to be gradually increased in intensity by means of a dial marked in volts.

The experiment was not in fact a "learning experiment,"

but rather a study to see how the subjects would react to being told to give someone else painful shocks. At "75 volts," the pretend-subject would give mild grunts. The reactions would be screams of "Get me out of here. I won't be in the experiment any longer. I refuse to go on," at "150 volts"; violent screams at "315 volts"; silence at "330 volts." The maximum level was "450 volts."

A group of thirty-nine psychiatrists were asked to predict in advance how far subjects from the Yale University student body would go. With almost complete agreement, their consensus was that only 4 percent would reach "300 volts," and that only a pathological fringe—fewer than 1 in 1000—would go to "450 volts."

In fact, over 60 percent of the Yale students went all the way. In Italy, South Africa, and Australia, the percentage was somewhat higher. In Munich, the percentage was 85 percent.

Although there was a very great deal of shock and discussion of how "sick" the subjects, and possibly the whole human race, were and the terrible implications this had for the future of our civilization, a major variable was ignored in this study— and the results were largely determined by it. This is the fact that the subjects were removed from their normal environments *before the study actually started* and placed in a very special one with different rules. The new rules were, in effect, "Forget everything you have been taught in the past. Forget your ethical standards and beliefs. Forget your long-range goals and aspirations. There is only one law or morality here—Obey the experimenter." By agreeing to be subjects in the experiment, the subjects agreed to obey these laws as long as they were in the laboratory. If the experiment had been titled "Behavior in Extreme Situations" (as was the famous paper on the concentration camps by Bruno Bettelheim), and the interpretations followed from the title, no one could have argued with its data.

The truth of this is demonstrated by further experiments, where the subjects had more free choice. When the subjects were told that *they* could choose the level of administered "shock" regardless of the number of mistakes the strapped-in "subjects" made, they chose the lowest level. Their average was "54 volts," far below the level of the first elicited response of "mild grunts," at "75 volts." And further study showed that no matter how badly the subjects were frustrated and made angry, they maintained the low level and did not increase it. These studies point to a far different interpretation of the Milgrim study. They show that it is a study of the limits of effect on the individual of being in the laboratory situation. And that these limits are far wider than we have usually accepted.

However, until the further studies were done and showed the basic fallacy of the Milgrim experiments, it seemed clear that the laboratory had shown that the degree of hostility and sadism in a college student population was far higher than had been expected, boding ill for the future of our species. This was an entirely false conclusion, due to the artificiality of the laboratory environment and not to the nature of the subjects.

The psychologist David Bannister has put it:

In order to behave like scientists we must construct situations in which our subjects . . . can behave as little like human beings as possible and we do this in order to allow ourselves to make statements about the nature of their humanity.[7]

There are very few situations in which human beings allow themselves to do with very little reservation exactly what they are told to do. But this is what we set up in an experiment. Psychologist Charles Tart has pointed out that the dominant psychological research tradition is the "Colonial Paradigm": passive subjects who are manipulated by a knowledgeable experimenter to produce results.

When we find ourselves in a situation where we must obey someone else and follow their rules—for example, the Army, a prison situation, or the like—we are usually aware that we are behaving atypically for us and that we would behave in quite other ways if we were free. Oddly, while the subject may be aware of this in a psychological experiment, it is rare that the experimenter is!

The artificiality and narrowness of the laboratory situation is hard to overstate. Typically it "forgets," for example, that one of the single most important facts about human beings is that they can understand and cooperate with each other. Any experiment that treats individuals in isolation—as a large percentage do—is too narrow, too distorting, too irrelevant to be valid. It is as if one tried to understand the laws of economics by studying the economic picture of a person living alone on an island. In the philosopher of science Karl Popper's words:

> Robinson Crusoe and his isolated individual economy can never be a useful model for any economy whose problems arise precisely from the economic interaction of individuals and groups.[8]

And yet we frequently try to make models of human behavior from the reactions of isolated individuals in a laboratory.

When we change the social situation of an individual, we change his behavior. When we place him in a completely artificial situation, we get behavior as far from his normal behavior as the sexual behavior of the rat in the laboratory cage is from what it is in the wild. A good analogy for laboratory studies of people is that of the Martian scientist who is fascinated by our airplanes and wants to know how they work. He takes one home with him and places it in his laboratory, which happens to be under water. Here, with great care, diligence, and attention to the rules of science, he examines it. He finds that it has moving parts, that it is held together by nuts and bolts (as our behavior is held together by reflexes, reflex chains, and so on)—and that is about all. How airplanes work, or what they are for, or how they function in their natural environment—on land and in air—escapes him. When we consider that any real contribution to our understanding of how humans work has escaped the experimental psychologists over the past century, the analogy does not seem to be such an unfair one.

The great error of Behaviorism was that it drew the wrong conclusions from the boring, endless, and ultimately fruitless "introspective" studies of the founder of experimental psychology, Wilhelm Wundt and his followers. The conclusion they drew was that you could not study the mental processes of human beings in the laboratory, so psychologists had better ignore them and study other things.

A more correct conclusion would have been that you cannot study *anything* of importance or interest about human beings in the laboratory, so psychologists had better study human beings in their natural state. However this conclusion was considered unthinkable—it ran directly counter to the discovery in the physical sciences that anything of importance in their fields of interest *could* be studied in a laboratory.

Further, it soon became clear that humans were poor subjects for Behavioristic experiments. Again, the wrong conclusion was drawn from this fact. Instead of asking if, perhaps, Behavioristic models did not apply to human beings, John B. Watson and his followers, down to and including B. F. Skinner, decided to find "better" subjects so that they could better understand human beings through the study of these. An analogy might be a group of scientists who live in Venice and want to study automobiles. Since they run so poorly on or under water and there are no roads available, the scientists decide to study canoes instead so that through them they can better understand automobiles.

The analogy is not a bad one. Canoes are about as similar to cars as rats are to human beings. On the one side, both are mammals. On the other, both are human-made objects that transport people faster and better than they could go themselves in the relevant terrain. Rats and canoes are easier and cheaper to obtain for experimental purposes than people and cars.

To state the above somewhat differently: early in its development psychology ran up against the fact that there are many events—that is, feelings and thoughts—that I can observe when they happen to me but not when they happen to anyone else. (To paraphrase Ludwig Wittgenstein, I cannot have a pain in *your* leg.) However, with its commitment to the methods of nineteenth-century physics, and its conviction that the methods used then were the only scientific methods, psychology decided that events that had only private access, rather than public access, could not be studied scientifically! The study of consciousness was, therefore, largely abandoned. The mechanistic hypothesis and the methods of the physical sciences were so much a part of the culture that anything that did not fit these systems of thought was labeled "unscientific;" to study them marked the researcher as not a scientist. Scientist and philosopher Michael Polanyi has pointed out that "All true scientific research starts with hitting on a deep and promising problem and this is one-half of the solution." The "deep and promising problem" of psychology was how to do research in an area where part of the data was open to public access and part was open only to private access. Unfortunately, this problem was never accepted as the basic methodological problem of psychology.

Around the turn of the century, and in the twenty or twenty-five years following, both philosophy and psychology abandoned the study of the nature of consciousness. Trying to be scientific, both disciplines retreated to the study of the trivia they felt they could study "scientifically."

The philosophers said that they only needed to study and understand the nature of language in order to solve all their problems and that the nature of mind was a problem of psychology. The psychologists said that they only needed to study and understand the basic elements that made up perception and behavior (as soon as they found out what these basic elements were) to solve all their problems and that the nature of mind was a problem of philosophy. Everyone felt very scientific and modern, and mountains of very scientific reports on trivia piled up in both fields—and that was about all.

In recent years, criticisms of the possibility of doing meaningful research in the laboratory, research that will lead to deeper understanding of the great problems of human life, have been increasing in frequency in the psychological journals. Book after book and paper after paper have raised the kinds of questions I have been describing in this chapter. Responses to these publications, defending the value and validity of the psychology laboratory, have also begun to appear.

The strongest defense of laboratory work in recent years, of which I am aware, is that of D. G. Mook, which appeared in the *American Psychologist* in 1983. He states that the purpose of laboratory investigation is to show what subjects will do *in a laboratory* and is not generalizable to life outside the laboratory.

> A misplaced preoccupation with external validity can lead us to dismiss good research for which generalization to real life is not intended or meaningful. . . . Our theory specifies what our subjects should do *in the laboratory*. Then we go to the laboratory and ask, Do they do it?[9]

If anyone is interested in behavior in highly artificial environments that cannot be generalized to real life, then, from Mook's point of view, they should become research psychologists. Those whose interests go beyond this should find other professions. I cannot quarrel with this, but as a defense of psychological laboratory research, it seems to be saying that a large part of its value is that it keeps psychologists off the streets, amused, and out of trouble.

We should also be aware that both individual and group psychotherapy present restrictive situations, lacking ecological validity. One must be extremely cautious about drawing inferences from what happens in therapy to human behavior in natural-life situations. No laboratory experiment is more artificial than making an appointment with a total stranger, walking into a strange office, and facing a person whom one has never met before, and being immediately expected to talk about the most personal and the most important things in one's life. Therapists tend to judge a patient quickly, on the basis of a very short acquaintance in a highly structured and artificial situation, and they tend to be remarkably resistant to changing this initial impression in the light of later experience. Many years ago Richard Renneker, a highly trained psychoanalyst, made films of the behavior of his colleagues through one-way mirrors he had installed (with their knowledge and cooperation) in their offices. Recording their behavior from the first session with a new patient until far along in the therapeutic process, he observed to his horror that they usually made up their minds about the structure and pathology of a particular patient in the first session, and that almost nothing the patient did or said thereafter could change their minds. When he brought his filmed demonstrations of this to his colleagues and asked for their help in remedying what was clearly a situation damaging to their work, they solved the problem by seeing to it that his research grant was abruptly taken away from him and that he was very shortly dismissed from the Chicago Psychoanalytic Institute in which he had achieved the high rank of Training Analyst.

We all know, that when we meet a new person in real life, it takes a long time to find out what is important about him, what the major thrusts of his personality and behavior are, and how he is *likely* to feel and act in a variety of situations. Therapists tend to understand this with people that they meet outside of their offices. Inside, however, they usually become so filled with the pride of their field that they forget it completely—in spite of the fact that they are meeting someone in a far more restricting, artificial, and distorting situation than if they met him or her in the street or in a social evening. I recall, for example, one patient who brought to the first session with a new therapist a dream of an atomic explosion in a subway. This convinced the therapist that the patient had a weak ego that could easily be disrupted. Although the patient had a strong and resilient ego that had stood up and continued to stand up under much stress, nothing that happened in the next four years of psychotherapy could convince the therapist that she was wrong and should reevaluate her opinion. Not only was the four-year process of therapy largely a waste of time and money, but much damage was done to the patient's life and feelings about himself.

(In view of the rigidity of most psychotherapists in staying firmly with their opinions [which are the opinions of the particular school in which they were trained about the nature of human beings and the consequent nature of "real" psychotherapy], in spite of their frequent failures with patients who do not fit their particular model, and in view of their rigidity in staying firmly with their opinion about the nature of this specific patient in spite of anything the patient may do to try to change their opinion, one is reminded of Woody Allen's question about fees to a psychoanalyst. Should they, he asked, be reported to the IRS as medical deductions or as religious contributions?)

Thirty and forty years ago there was much more understanding of this in the profession of psychotherapy; we used to try to hold our impressions and check them against projective tests. We waited until we could test our initial impressions against those made with the use of another instrument, such as the Rorschach Test or the Thematic Apperception Test. In addition, many clinics made available the additional tool of a good social work interview made from a different viewpoint from our own, usually therapeutic, investigations. This, at least, gave us the chance to look for common factors in the patient's behavior in *two* and sometimes *three* distorting situations and so tremendously increased our chances of more valid understanding. Today, however, the arrogance and self-confidence of psychotherapists has grown so great that they prefer to make complete judgments about another human being on the basis of what that person does in the course of one or two hours (or fifty-minute periods), in as artificial a situation as is possible to find on this planet. Besides, there is so much more money and prestige in being a therapist than there is in giving projective tests or functioning as a social worker that—with the exception of a few good clinics and teaching centers—these functions have been largely abandoned as everyone qualified to do them scrambles to become a therapist.

If, in the majority of modern clinics and hospitals psychiatric services, a psychiatrist asks a psychologist for a projective test on a patient, or asks a social worker for a social work workup, the response is likely to be a superior sniff and an insulted "I don't do that sort of thing. *I* am a therapist."

Certainly, in recent years, there have been reactions to the psychotherapeutic problems I have been describing here. Family therapy, the newest fashion in psychotherapy, is a beginning of the revolution against the idea that a person can be meaningfully understood apart from his ecology, his environment, and the relationships that make up so large a part of these. If it were not inconvenient for the therapists, we would certainly by this time have them doing family therapy in people's homes so that they could see their patients function in an even more natural environment.

The idea that our procedures are dictated in part by the therapist's need for comfort and prestige should not be seen as limited to therapists alone. For many years, a woman in childbirth half leaned back into a special chair while the physician kneeled at her feet to receive the baby. As many modern midwives will attest, this was a far superior position for the woman than the more-widely-used-today position of flat-on-her-back-with-the-physician-standing-upright. However, the kneeling position was adjudged to be denigrating of the dignity of the physician and so was abandoned by them—to the detriment and discomfort of women in labor.

Seymour Sarason, one of our most brilliant and wide-ranging psychologists, has shown, more than anyone else, how little psychologists, both of the research and of the clinical variety, have considered themselves part of a social and cultural process and how this lack of understanding of themselves in a context has damaged and invalidated their work. Sarason points out in some detail that psychology studied individuals and largely ignored the social order that shaped and constantly influenced them. Further, he notes that psychologists paid little attention to the fact that they themselves were shaped by their society and so their view of the nature of man, their image of what a human being is, their theories about psychology, came from it. They did not try to look behind the views and assumptions of the society in which they grew up. His rich and colorful analyses of these concepts deserve careful reading by anyone who cares about the field of psychology.[10]

To summarize briefly: both the laboratory and the psychotherapy office are highly distorting and artificial situations. People's behavior in either of these generally bears very little relationship to their behavior in real life, and extrapolations *to this person* from *this patient* or from *this experimental subject* are extremely dubious.

There is no reason to conclude from this chapter that there is no place for laboratory work in psychology. There is a real place—but only as part of a science designed to study human beings and not as part of a science originally designed to study physical objects like cams and gears and driveshafts. Later in this book, I will describe the kind of science I am referring to and show the place of the laboratory in it. Those who have used this method as it was originally developed by Wilhelm Dilthey, Ernest Rénan, and Wilhelm Windelband, and who have refined it further—people like Robin Collingwood and Heinrich Rickert in the field of history, Konrad Lorenz and Nikolaus Tinbergen in ethology, and Freud in psychiatry—have made real advances, not the puerile, pitiful, and trivial advances that have come from the psychology laboratories.[11]

5

NUMBERS AND HUMAN FEELINGS

The third general principle that psychology took from nineteenth-century science is that everything in the cosmos is quantitative and—if you wish to be scientific—must be approached through measurement and precise numbers. Until, goes this viewpoint, you can state something numerically, you have not attained a scientific understanding of it. Further, once you have quantified your material correctly, you should be able to predict how it will behave in the future. Lack of predictability means you have not yet attained any scientific understanding of your subject.

The basic requirement for publication in academic psychology has been what is called "the CGS trick"—you must be able to state your results in centimeters, grams, or seconds.[1] The CGS standard was widely used, although not much discussed, in academic research. The result was that anything that could not be described in this way—which meant anything important or meaningful in human life—was not studied or even looked at very much. Only the trivial tended to be publishable in the journals. With a "publish or perish" system in academia, this led in an obvious and inevitable direction.

The nineteenth-century maxim "Everything that exists, exists in some measure" has some truth in it, but when we come to human thought and feeling, to our inner life, this "measure" cannot be reduced to numbers. How can you tell me in numbers, quantify, reduce to units, the effect on you of your first love, the death of a parent, the birth of your first child, your first deeply religious experience? Or what happened to you the first time you really *heard* Beethoven's "Appassionata" or *saw* Picasso's *Guernica?*

The philosopher Ernst Cassirer took his ten-year-old daughter Anna to see *The Marriage of Figaro.* It was her first opera. When she came out, it seemed to her that the whole world had changed. Her beloved Berlin looked very different. Seventy years later she still remembered this as a major experience in her life. How would you quantify this incident and its effect on her?

Obviously the important aspects of human life are not describable in numbers or reducible to units. But—in academic psychology—we tried. When it became obvious to us that meaningful things, such as those mentioned above, could not be quantified, we were faced with a tremendous and far-reaching choice. On the one hand, we could give up our theory in the face of the facts and begin to study human beings in a way related to what we had observed—a nonquantitative way. Or, on the other hand, we could maintain our theory, and our illusions that we were being "scientific," by ignoring the facts and continuing to do quantitative research. The only way we could do this was to study only unimportant and trivial aspects of being human. For these aspects we could obtain nice numbers and even a few very limited laws. We found that we could devise some general rules for the best way of learning lists of nonsense syllables—but none for learning no-nonsense facts. Thus there are rules for the best way of spacing, to best remember, forty syllables such as *bam, fet, til, kep,* and *hak,* but none for learning and remembering that your first child is a girl, that the armistice has been signed and the war is over, or that there is an atom bomb and humanity is at peril.

The idea and basic methodology for quantifying activity came into psychology through the work of Carl Weber and Gustav Fechner. Every intermediate psychology student knows of the Weber-Fechner Function, the first general equation for converting human activity into numbers. Hardly anyone except Fechner noticed that it only applied to very simple human activities and then only over a narrow range of them. It is useful in predicting how accurately a person will gauge whether or not two weights are equal, provided the weights are not too light or too heavy. Fechner himself wrote a series of essays under the name of Dr. Mises satirizing mechanical science. In these he makes plain that to try to quantify human psychology is to repudiate it and to retreat completely from human thought and feeling. So great, however, was the influence of the physical sciences that Fechner is remembered only for the kind of work he thought useless and hopeless.

We made vast efforts to quantify all inner and outer human activity and failed. We devised the names of units of feelings (the unit of joy is the *Exuberant;* the unit of pain is the *Dol,* from the French *douleur)*, but found it impossible to assign numbers to these units.

Access to consciousness, finally, is private rather than public. "It is obvious," wrote the psychologist Franz Brentano, "that no mental phenomena can be perceived by more than one person." We have, on the contrary, public access to observables, data, in the sensory realm. You and I can agree or disagree on the length of a table; we can measure it and come to an agreement as to how long it is. We can even agree on what method to use to solve our disagreement if there is one— a yardstick, or a pulse of coherent light, or the decision of an "objective" observer. But only *I* can observe the processes in my own consciousness. *We* cannot disagree about whether or not I feel sad. We can find no way for you to observe my sadness, and "objective observer" is a meaningless term here. Where would we find him and what would he do? Hugo Munsterberg (who first organized Harvard University's psychology laboratory), in 1899, regarded this as one of the central facts of psychology. He defined "physical" as "all that is a possible object for every subject," and "psychical" as "all that is a possible object for one subject only."

It is partly for this reason that events in consciousness are, *in principle*, nonquantifiable. If I cannot observe your joy and you cannot observe mine, then how can we ever agree on how much joy constitutes one "exuberant"? And if I say that I have two "dols" of pain in my toothache, how can you ever know how much pain that signifies? "Now it is the essence of mental things," wrote the philosopher Henri Bergson, "that they do not lend themselves to measurement."

> *You cannot have a ton of love (in spite of the way girls used to sign their letters) or a yard of hate or a gallon of numinous awe; but love and hate and awe are just as real as a ton of flour or a yard of linen or a gallon of petrol, more real indeed, because they have immediate significance, they are not simply means to ends like making bread, a pillow case or haste.*[2]

I may describe a particular feeling I have today as "more" or "much more," "less" or "much less" than a similar feeling I had yesterday, but that is about all I can do. "It is the mark of a properly trained mind to look for a degree of precision that is appropriate to the subject matter, and only to the degree that the nature of each allows," wrote Aristotle in his *Nicomachean Ethics*.

We can, of course, measure how much *action* an emotion leads to. This, however, does not quantify our feeling, but our response to it. These are fundamentally different things; the feeling itself is only one factor among many that determine the response. If, in the words of the old cigarette advertisement, I'd walk a mile for a Camel, it is not only my feeling of desire for a cigarette that determines whether or not I set out on the hike;

it is also my general feelings of strength or fatigue, whether or not I enjoy walking, my other plans for the next hour, and whether or not I have read the latest report on smoking and lung cancer. If I walk one mile for a cigarette and you walk two miles, this does not mean that your desire (or addiction) is twice as great as mine, but only that your response is. Not only might you feel the need for exercise more than I; I might not like giving in to my own desires as much as you. Besides, my feet might hurt.

Another finding as we explore the realm of consciousness is that the situation is always changing and never repeats itself. *"No state of consciousness,"* wrote William James, *"once gone, can recur and be identical with what it was before. . . ."* (italics his). James continues: "A permanently existing idea . . . which makes its appearance before the flashlight of consciousness at periodic intervals is as mythical as the Jack of Spades."[3]

This concept that the situation never repeats itself seems surprising and unlikely at first, accustomed as we are to the model of the physical sciences (created and appropriate for the realm of experience accessible to the senses) by means of which a situation can be re-created and an experiment repeated. I can make a repeatable experiment in these fields because I can isolate a specific system of interesting events and create this system again and again in the same manner. There are, however, a number of fields in which this cannot be done. As Henri Bergson put it:

> *History does not repeat itself. The battle of Austerlitz was fought once and it will never be fought again. It being impossible that the same historical conditions should ever be reproduced, the same historic fact cannot be repeated: and as a law expresses necessarily that to certain causes, always the same, there will correspond an effect, also always the same, history strictly speaking has no bearing on laws, but on particular facts, and on the no less particular circumstances which brought them to pass.*[4]

In a fascinating essay, Søren Kierkegaard recounts his attempt to find an example of exact repetition in life. Search as he might through places he had lived in before, he could not find one. His conclusion: "There is no such thing as repetition."

What is true in the realm in which history is studied is as true in the realm of consciousness. This is one reason that it is not possible, in principle, to produce a repeatable experiment in psychology any more than it is in history. Even if a psychological experiment is repeated by the same scientist he—as the parapsychologist Robert Brier has pointed out—is doing it for the second time. If it is done by a different scientist, there is also a major difference. (The same problem applies to the subjects in the experiments.) The question of repeatability in science is not one of exact repetition, but of which differences make a difference. In certain fields—such as chemistry—the difference between experimenters—whether, for instance, the experimenter is a virgin, in terms of *this* experiment, does not make a difference. In fields involving consciousness, however, they make a real difference. In certain fields, repeatability of experiments is a possible and a useful criterion of method. In other fields it is neither a useful concept nor a possible procedure. As Arthur Koestler put it:

> One of the cornerstones of scientific methodology is the formula ceteris paribus—"other things being equal." But other things are never equal where human subjects are concerned . . . ask any writer, painter or scientist to define the precise conditions under which the creative spark will repeatedly and predictably ignite the vapours in his mind![5]

Of equal importance here is the fact that you can make accurate predictions about how individual entities behave only when you have the same events repeated over and over again so you can test your laws against observations. The "same events" are events where the differences between them make no difference. Two round iron balls, weighing one pound each rolling down a smooth plane inclined at twenty-two degrees, are certainly two *different* iron balls. However, for the purpose of developing a general law from which to make predictions, the differences make no difference. Both roll down the inclined plane with no appreciable differences in speed.

However, the speed with which two adult humans (or even more, two children) walk from home to work (or to school) or, to sound scientific, from point A to point B, is determined by a wide variety of factors. These certainly include their structure (for example, length of legs), the immediate surrounding situation (smoothness of terrain, direction and speed of wind), and their knowledge of, feelings about, and definition of, the reasons they are moving and what awaits them when they arrive. The list of factors included here is very large, ranging from how they feel about their job and workplace, their general philosophy and their mood of the moment, knowledge, beliefs about themselves, others and the world in general. All these differences do make a difference, and so we cannot predict from the first individual's speed of approaching his office how fast the second will walk. And since these factors and their relative intensity change from one time to the next, we cannot predict how fast he will walk tomorrow from how fast Joe walks today.

A "repeatable experiment" in the realm of consciousness tells us we are dealing with a damaged person. If, in a free-association test, every time we give the word *black* the subject replies *white*, and we can repeat this indefinitely (without ever getting a response like *boring*, for example), we know that something is wrong. We know that this person is so damaged that his response pattern is frozen, that he is so emotionally tied up or so heavily conditioned that the natural response is no longer present.

An artist who, standing in the same spot at the same time of day, painted exactly the same picture over and over again would be regarded as an extremely damaged person. We would expect a camera to exactly reproduce the same thing under the same conditions, but not an artist. If, for example, we look at the repeated paintings by van Gogh of the wheat fields at Arles, or at Cézanne's repeated paintings of Mont Sainte-Victorie, we see that each one is a completely distinct and very different painting. There is no repetition. At any one of the times that van Gogh or Cézanne set up his easel, it would have been impossible in principle to predict what the new painting was going to look like.

For real individual human beings we cannot predict what is going to happen in their consciousness or what their molar (large-scale, meaningful) behavior will be. We can no more predict what the next novel of a writer will be on the basis of his previous novels than we could have predicted what Beethoven's Ninth Symphony would be like after hearing its eight forerunners. (We would, for example, be certain that there would be no voices in it.) Human beings are nonpredictable in principle. Only papier-mâché characters can be predicted. We can make 100-percent accurate predictions that Tom Swift, Tarzan, and James Bond will emerge triumphant from their next adventure, not so for Captain Cook, Al Capone, or Albert Einstein.

A prediction about molar human behavior, or conscious activity, is a prediction about a single event. Such an event can never be repeated since the conditions that are important can never be exactly the same. As the psychologist T. R. Sarbin has shown so clearly, such a prediction, if made, is nonverifiable (or nonfalsifiable) in principle. If I say that the chances are one in six that Jones will commit suicide within a year, how is such a statement to be confirmed or shown to be false? If Jones commits suicide (or if he does not) the result is equally compatible with my statement, *and* with the statement "The chances are one in two that Jones will commit suicide within a year," or the statement that the chances are one in ten. Probability statements about a single event are nonverifiable.

This applies to statistical predictions. The problem is the same when we attempt to make absolute predictions in the realm of molar behavior or in the realm of consciousness. An absolute prediction needs a general law, and no laws can be made if the situation cannot be repeated with the important variables held constant. This cannot be done in these realms.

With no absolute laws (for example, Boyle's Law) we cannot make absolute predictions. In the words of Wilhelm Wundt: "There is no psychological law to which the exceptions are not more numerous than the agreements."

In the realm of large numbers of people, on the other hand, I *can* make statistical predictions. From what I know of present social conditions and engineers, I predict that at the next annual convention of the American Association of Electrical Engineers, between 36 and 42 percent of the attendees will wear ties to meetings in the morning. This prediction I can check out. But I cannot predict in the realm of specific individuals, and if I do, my predictions only *sound* as if they had any meaning. There is no way that I can check them. If I say that there is a 40-percent chance that the twenty-first engineer who comes into the registration hall on Tuesday morning will be wearing a tie, am I actually saying *anything*? I stand at the entrance hall, let twenty engineers pass and look at the twenty-first, an engineer named Ralph Stone. He is wearing a tie. Is my prediction borne out? It is impossible to tell. I can make a guess as to whether or not Stone will be wearing a tie, and I can be correct or not. But there are no laws by means of which I can make a specific prediction about an individual event or person. And a statistical prediction has no meaning in this realm.

The molar behavior of groups of individuals is in a different realm of experience from the molar behavior of one person. This is demonstrated by the successful prediction of actuarial statistics versus the impossibility of predicting the behavior of any one individual. As quantum mechanics has demonstrated, there is no paradox involved here. In different realms, different things are possible and different things are impossible. With one particle or person I can, *at best,* make a pretty fair "guesstimate": with large numbers of either, I can predict with very great accuracy.

In a chemistry (or any other domain in the sensory realm) experiment, if absolute repeatability does *not* occur (that is, if the match does not light the magnesium strip each time), we know that something is very wrong. In the realm of consciousness, if absolute repeatability *does* occur, we know that some-thing is very wrong.

A science of entities that are quantifiable in nature is also a science that can *predict* future actions and reactions of the entities it studies. This is a crucial point because so many sci-entists believe that the hallmark of a real science is how accu-rately it can predict the future. If this criterion is accepted as valid, neither psychology nor history can ever be acceptable in the roster of sciences.

Social scientists look on astronomy (nineteenth-century style) as the ideal and model. Its exact predictions are our goal. We say, in effect, "If astronomy can predict eclipses so accu-rately, some day we will be able to predict national revolutions to the day and hour of their occurrence."

Social scientists consider one part of astronomy in partic-ular—Celestial Dynamics in the solar system. This is the theory of motions and events as determined by physical forces. We look forward to and expect of ourselves a Social Dynamics—a theory of social movement and occurrences as determined by historical and psychological forces.

But to do this, we would have to know how individuals in the future will interpret and react to social and historical situ-ations. Since they will do this on the basis of information that they will have in the future, we would have to know now what that information will be. In other words, we would have to know now what information will be available in the future. This is impossible on the face of it. How can we tell how a person will interpret a situation when he or she will have in-formation and experience we do not and can not have?

The knowledge of a planet does not change. Its response to other forces therefore does not change. Its response to these forces will be the same in the future as it is now. This is not true of human beings, or even of animals in the wild.

The concept that science is a means of predicting what will happen in the future is, perhaps, the one that most clearly shows the difference between different *kinds* of science. This notion—that we are not really being scientific until we can accurately predict what is going to occur—is fine and necessary for mechanical engineers. It is a source of confusion and depression for psychologists.

One reason is that human behavior and consciousness do not vary with the situation, but with how the individual defines and interprets the situation—two very different things.

Karl Popper defines *historicism* as "an approach to the social sciences which assumes that *historical prediction* is their principal aim."[6]

The essence of this idea is that a theory of history (for example, Marxism) predicts the future. However, our behavior is based always on our knowledge. It is impossible in principle to predict what we will know in the future. We cannot predict what a man or a culture will know in times to come. The past can be "explained" or comprehended; we can be aware of what a man or a culture knew or believed in the past. But what will we or they know or believe in the future?

The total failure of Marxism (the major example of *historicism*) to predict its own future—in such crucial areas as the rise of fascism, the Stalin era, and the events of 1989–90 in Eastern Europe—shows the total bankruptcy of this idea.

What is true for the study of history is true for the study of the individual. Both problems have the same structure; the study of the individual is simply the study of the smallest valid historical unit, the smallest "group."

How a steam engine behaves—what it does—depends on its structure and the situation around it. How a human being behaves depends on his structure, the situation around him, *and how he defines it.* His definition is partly based on his knowledge. Popper puts it quite bluntly:

> There can be no scientific theory of historical development serving as a basis for historical prediction. . . . Our behavior and history are governed by our knowledge. If there is such a thing as growing human knowledge, then we cannot anticipate today what we shall only know tomorrow. . . .
> No scientific predictor, *whether a human scientist or a*

calculating machine, can scientifically predict by scientific methods its own future knowledge.[7]

What a person will know in the future is, in principle, impossible to predict. Therefore his definitions and consequent actions are impossible to predict. This is true of individuals and entire cultures. The science of futurology and the science of phrenology are about equal in validity.

Compounding the problem is that we feel we *should* be able to predict human behavior. This partly comes from a time before modern anthropology when it was felt that there was only one, real human nature—although primitive groups or groups of past periods might not yet have attained it. This is a trap that the historian falls into far less frequently than the psychologist. Anyone who has studied the Visigoths and the Romans, the Sioux and the Navaho, or even the Hippies of the 1960s and the Yuppies of the 1980s realizes that human nature differs to a very considerable extent from place to place and time to time. A Hopi sheepherder, a knight of the First Crusade, a 1980 Wall Street broker, and a laboratory psychologist live in different worlds with different definitions of space, time, and honor, different life goals, different views of love and the meaning of death.

Every historian knows that the Spartans and the Phoenicians thought in very different ways and lived in different universes and that no "law of human nature" could encompass both. People think in different ways in different cultures in different times. There is no "one way all human beings respond to this . . ." There are recurrent patterns in particular social periods—the way feudal barons tended to think in the medieval period, for example—but when the culture changes, so do these repetitions.

Of crucial importance in the development of an individual, a nation, or a race are the *unique* events, the events that never can repeat: one's birth, one's first love, the first war for independence from foreign rule, the discovery of the value of fire. What are we to say of a science that cannot deal with nonrepeatable events, that insists that the hallmark of its being is predictability? We can only say that such a science may indeed be of vast value in realms where all events are repeatable, that is, in physics or mechanics, but is completely misplaced and useless in realms where this is not so.

This is not new knowledge: Immanuel Kant, deeply concerned and involved with the rules of pure reason, pointed out that ". . . into all acts of judgment there enters, and must enter, a personal decision that cannot be accounted for by any rules."[8] He says that this is inscrutable to reason. Here is a clear indication, by Kant, of the impossibility of predicting human behavior by scientific laws. Reason ultimately bows to decisions that cannot be accounted for by reason.

Hegel pointed out that the kind of regularities and lawful recurrences that are found in the natural world do not occur in the mind or spirit.

Both the art historian and critic Benedetto Croce and the historian R. G. Collingwood wanted to ensure that history was released from "its state of pupilage to the natural sciences." They repeatedly pointed out the falseness of the "assumption that historical occurrences could be subsumed under, or explained in terms of, universal laws of the sort that played an essential part in scientific interpretation of inanimate knowledge." As Collingwood put it: "The historian has no gift of prophecy, and knows it; the historical study of mind, therefore, can neither forestall the future developments of human thought nor legislate it."

One area in which people accepted the idea that we could validly assign numbers to important aspects of human life and then predict behavior from this number was in the field of intelligence.

The concept of the *IQ* was first invented by the psychologist William Stern when he was, in his words, "a very young man." Stern's deepest wish in his later years was to introduce the concept of the Person and Personalistic Psychology in America in order "to counteract the pernicious effect of my earlier invention, the I.Q."[9]

The concept of the IQ was more technically developed in the early twentieth century by Alfred Binet and Theodore Simon. Here was the first time we had techniques to *define numerically* a meaningful part of human personality; we felt very scientific. The Binet-Simon Intelligence test was widely diffused and used and variations of all kinds were made of it.

The IQ field today is in such a mess that in 1984 the police in New York came up with a rather original solution to the problems it raised. Black and Hispanic policemen had claimed that the intelligence tests used for sergeants ratings were unfair to them and demanded a new one. They were given permission to commission a new test, and they selected a company to design one for them. They then examined and approved the result. However, the new test also passed a higher percentage of Caucasian than it did of black and Hispanic applicants. After the test had been given, they and the organization that had selected the company doing the design reported that the test was "fair," but that the *results* were discriminating and that the test should be scrapped!

In the early 1970s, Simon (to the great surprise of most psychologists, who had assumed that he was long dead) wrote a letter to the major psychology journal, *The American Psychologist.* He deplored the widespread use of, and the importance given to, what he described as a minor and unimportant tool that he and Binet had devised to help teachers check some of their impressions of students in certain types of difficulty. It should not, wrote the pioneer, be used for anything else.

Sixty years of intelligence testing of children have taught us very little, if anything, about children that we did not already know. Intelligence testing has, however, made very real contributions to statistical theory that are not applicable to any specific child. It has also damaged a great many children who believed in the validity of the concept or whose parents or teachers did.

So far as I know, the only truly intelligent use made of the concept was in the United States Army in World War II. They used a very good group intelligence test, the Army General Classification Test (AGCT), to indicate that *this* soldier, at *this* time of his life, in the presence of sufficient motivation, leadership, and various personality and experience categories, could successfully pass through certain Army schools. The qualifiers were always very clear. If a concept is so basically flawed that just about the only organization using it intelligently is the Army, everyone else had better be pretty careful with it.

There is no question but that the IQ tests and testers have flunked their "examinations." The purpose of their work was to show that they could predict behavior. They could not. Further, when examined as a group, the test designers violently disagreed on what they were testing. As Seymour Sarason has pointed out, "The concept of intelligence is a social invention, inevitably reflecting social time and place, not a 'thing' in an individual."[10] A person's pancreas or his brain may have a definite size. Not his intelligence.

Further, as the IQ became so popular and so widely accepted, it often had unlooked-for effects on public policy. When H. H. Goddard (of Jukes and Kallikaks fame) tested immigrants at Ellis Island with the Binet-Simon Intelligence Test, he found that 83 percent of Jews, 80 percent of Hungarians, 79 percent of Italians, and 87 percent of Russians were feebleminded. These results had a strong effect on the immigration policies of the United States.

It would be easy to continue to point out that in reifying (making an abstract concept concrete and "real") intelligence, in making it a "thing" to which we could assign numbers, we have done very little good and much harm, that we have violated the very thing we claimed to be studying. However, this would be uninteresting. Rather, let us take a true and simple concrete example. A five-year-old child was given an IQ test in school. At home afterward her mother asked her how it had gone. "Oh," she said, "it was easy except for one question that was too hard. The teacher told me to draw a lion between the picture of a table and the picture of a chair. I can't draw a lion so I drew a daisy." The mother said, "I think she meant draw a line." "Oh, no," replied the five-year-old, "that would have been too easy." (This is the same child who, when asked in the test to complete the series "The fox ate the three little rabbits. The fox ate the four little rabbits. The fox ate the five little rabbits. The fox ate the dash little rabbits," responded with the word *poor.*)

Here is what is real, important, unique about human life— the creative, the compassionate—leading to a wrong response on intelligence test questions. Which do you consider to be of more value, to contain more hope for our species: the response "six" or the response "poor"? The test manual says otherwise.

6

MAKING A MODEL
OF MAN

The fourth idea that psychology took from the physical sciences as a basic concept was that you can—and for real understanding, you *must*—make a model, a metaphor, for anything you are studying. Any entity, or class of occurrences, can be better understood as a metaphor and then can be studied and researched as such. In part, this came from the experience of Descartes and others that much of the action of mechanical objects could be best understood through examining graphs, charts, and tables of mathematical formulas. If, for example, as Descartes found, you wished to teach artillerymen how to charge and elevate their cannons so as to hit a specific target, you gave them mathematical tables to use. They did much better looking at these than they did looking at the target.

This concept—that scientific understanding of an entity, event, or process is increased by making a model of it and then manipulating the model—is both subtle and profound. It has been seen all through the scientific field since the seventeenth century. An atom is modeled as a miniature solar system. An electron is modeled as a wave or a particle. The evolution of a species is visualized as a tree with dividing branches. The development of a civilization is modeled on the seasons of the year. To a Marxist, the evolution of society is that of a machine, inexorably developing on lines as predetermined as those of a clock.

This concept has been of great value in the field of molar physics and of mechanics generally. Here the mechanical model was applied and, once it was understood, accurately described the phenomena we were dealing with. The tremendous success of physics and mechanics in the nineteenth century was largely fostered by the use of the mechanical model *in the fields in which it was valid.*

In the human sciences, however, it is a different matter. Here the use of models has had an entirely opposite effect. Any model we have used for human beings has slowed and impeded our progress. The technique, so useful in physics, has not been applicable to our work.

One psychologist, Albert Chapanis, put it:

Like Descartes, modellists seem to be inspired by the latest physical theories and playthings. Newton's mechanics brought forth models of man which treated him simply as a machine made up of levers and similar linkages. Watt's steam engine and the development of thermodynamics produced models of man which viewed him as nothing but a complicated heat engine. When servo-mechanisms mushroomed during World War 2, we heard that man is nothing but a servo system. Somewhat more recently communication theory has been translated into models which purport to show that man is only an information handling system. [1]

A recent quotation in the journal *Advances* said this another way:

CAVEAT EMPTOR:
THE BRAIN IS NOT A PIECE OF TECHNOLOGY

"Because we don't understand the brain very well we're constantly tempted to use the latest technology as a model for trying to understand it.

"In my childhood we were always assured that the brain was a telephone switchboard ('What else could it be?') And I was amused to see that Sherrington, the great British neuroscientist, thought that the brain worked like a telegraph system. Freud often compared the brain to hydraulic and electro-magnetic systems. Leibniz compared it to a mill, and now, obviously, the metaphor is the digital computer. . . .

"The computer is probably no better and no worse as a metaphor for the brain than earlier mechanical metaphors. We learn as much about the brain by saying it's a computer as we do by saying it's a telephone switchboard, a telegraph system, a water pump, or a steam engine."

—John Searle, *"Minds, Brains, and Science,"*
The 1984 Reith Lectures.[2]

The simplicity of the various images of man that have been used by psychologists, and the fact that they have very little (or nothing) to do with human experience, demonstrates how psychologists have been looking for human beings everywhere except where they are. There is the old teaching story of the Sufis concerning the man who spent the night searching on the ground under a lamppost. When a friend asked him what he was doing, he said that he was searching for the keys to his house. After helping him search for some time, the friend asked him if he was certain he had lost them under the lamppost. "Oh no," said the man, "I lost them at home, but there is more light here."

There is only *apparently* more light where the psychologists have been searching for man. And he is not likely to be found in the same place the physical sciences find what they are looking for. Meister Eckhart once said that if you are searching for God, you should look in the place you lost Him. We might legitimately paraphrase this by saying that if you are searching for man, look where you lost him. Or, at least, in the natural environment where he is to be found.

Models only work for the simplest and most trivial aspects of human activity and consciousness. Given anything more meaningful and more important than the extinction of a conditioned eye-blink, they stop working. We, as a science, have refused to accept that the correct model of a human being is a human being. There is no reason not to be anthropomorphic when we are studying anthropos. You, I, Iago, and Mr. George Babbitt are not rats, computers, or the hyphen between a stimulus and a response, and to try to explain us as such is to look at an outmoded theory of science, not the data of our field.

A computer is a brain to the same degree that the Palomar telescope is an eye or a bulldozer is a muscle. Or vice versa.

It is interesting to note that every scientist who advocates a particular model leaves out one human being as an exception. Each says: "All humans behave as they do because they are a rat or a telephone exchange or a computer. But *I* write this book or give this lecture for entirely different reasons—*I* do it because I am a human being with intelligence and free will and altruistic motives."

And, of course, they must do this for two reasons. First, their *experience* tells them that they are not a hyphen between a stimulus and response operating purely because of conditioning chains. Second, because if they did not offer themselves as exceptions, who would pay any attention to them? If a B. F. Skinner wrote that his book said what it said because of his early or recent conditioning, why should we buy the book or pay any attention to it? After all, if he had been differently conditioned, we reason, he would have written something different.

Men love their wives, a speaker will state, because of cultural training, Oedipal displacement, or because they were accidentally conditioned to some of their wife's characteristics and therefore emit loving behavior. I, however, he will imply, love my wife because she is so lovable. Again the speaker has two reasons for this qualification. First, this is his actual experience. Second, he wants to be able to go home after the speech.

No historian, philosopher, or psychologist ever described his own research as due to a certain aspect of the class struggle, the need of his culture to dispose of excess productivity, or an inferiority complex. It is only the behavior of *others* that is determined by these motives. (It is easy to be reminded here of the psychoanalyst who, sitting in front of a wall of books, assures his patient that no one ever learned anything of importance, anything that changed his behavior to any significant degree, from books. Or the French existentialist philosopher, writing book after book all with the same theme—that human beings cannot communicate with each other.)

The strange thing about all this is that we accept as reasonable in the mouths of psychologists talking about nonpsychologists what we would consider psychotic in the mouths of nonpsychologists talking about themselves. And—to carry this very peculiar behavior on our part one step further—we accept as reasonable and worthy of consideration a psychologist saying certain things about others, but would consider it very pathological behavior if he said the same things about himself.

To illustrate this, let us suppose a Behavioristic psychologist has written many papers proving that human beings have no free will and are controlled by their early and late conditioning. Now let us suppose that this person said, in ordinary conversation, that he himself was a machine, controlled by forces and events that he was often not consciously aware of, and that he had no choice over what he said or how he said it. And further, let us suppose he said that he was a machine talking to other machines (by which he meant his audience) and that none of these machines had any control over their behavior, but all were controlled by these accidental and random forces.

We would certainly consider this person seriously deranged. However, if he only discussed all other human beings who were not in the room and described them in these terms, we might consider him a legitimate scientist.

One wonders who "emits" the stranger and sicker behavior—the Behavioristic psychologists or those who take them seriously.

Each time we invent a new model, or an old one again becomes chic, we are tempted (and generally give in to the temptation) to use it as a total explanatory system. The reflex, the birth order, the brain-as-computer, the mind-as-hydraulic-pump, the complex, the body-type, the exact-time-and-place-of-birth, the drive to self-realization, the human-as-white-rat, from time to time, all seem to serve us as ways to explain everything about human consciousness and behavior. Human beings tend to be as provincial in time as they are in space. And each time we do this, we do violence to the state of being human and to the person we are describing. I can discuss Oedipus, Richard the Lionheart, Robert E. Lee, Baron Richthofen, and Abraham Lincoln in any of these terms. However, when I am finished all I have is a flat two-dimensional picture. The *person* is lost.

We have developed what psychologist Gordon Allport described as a "contempt for the psychic surface of life." There is always for us a deeper and hidden meaning. Isaiah Berlin, the philosopher and economist, wrote of:

> . . . the schools of thought which look upon human activity as being largely caused by occult and inescapable forces of which explicit social beliefs and theories are rationalizations—disguises to be penetrated and exposed. This is the heritage of marxism, of depth psychology, of the sociology of Pareto or Simmel or Mannheim . . .[3]

In Joe Miller's Joke Book, an eighteenth-century collection of jokes, old when printed, is "Why does a chicken cross the road?" The answer, of course, is "To get to the other side." Think, however, of the answer the Behavioristic psychologist would give to the question! Or other learning theorists, or the Marxist, the astrologer, or the depth psychologist. And if these answers are given to the chicken, then what about Columbus and the Atlantic?

The basic fact is that models make good tools, but poor masters. I can view Columbus as the blind tool of a capitalistic system that needed more raw materials and therefore extruded explorers from the central land-mass of Europe. I can view him as driven by a compensation for an inferiority complex related to his family and his sibling position. I can see his behavior as impelled by the fact he was a male Gemini (or whatever sign he was born under). But if I wish to comprehend Christopher Columbus and why he persevered in the face of overwhelming discouragement and pain, then I must not lose the man in frames of reference that apply only to small parts of him. I must feel his feelings, see his vision, dream his dreams. I must conceptualize him as a human being like myself, not as a computer delivering its programming or a pigeon acting out its conditioning: Nor as a large upright rat, a servomechanism, a hologram, a telephone switchboard, or a flowering plant.

When Shylock finishes his great speech ("If you prick us, do we not bleed?"), we know him for another human being and we comprehend a little more what that means and what human beings can feel, suffer, and do. We do not, at that moment, view him as a mechanism acting blindly and automatically in the grip of an Adlerian drive-to-power, a Freudian reaction-formation-to-passive-drives, an Existentialist struggle-for-meaning, a Humanistic will-to-become, or as a Behavioristic machine responding to conditioning. And *this* is the reason that *The Merchant of Venice* contains more real psychology than shelf after shelf of psychology textbooks.

Another aspect of this difficulty with a model of a human being is that once we have one, we design our research on the basis of it. And thereby reinforce it. If I see man as a large, upright white rat, I will design studies that deal with ratlike characteristics, and the result of these studies will be that research shows man having ratlike characteristics and so on.

If, however, I go in the opposite direction and use a model

of man as a loving and altruistic goal-seeker (until unfortunate socializing and educational experiences tie him up in knots and make him act in hostile ways), see him as a sort of Ferdinand the Bull who *really* only wants to smell the flowers, then I will design experiments that show these characteristics and reinforce my own views. I will miss completely the complexity and the dark side of humanity. In both of these cases—and in all other models—we leave out a large part of the human being. The only model for anthropos is anthropos.

No experienced nursery school teacher, or other early-childhood educator working closely with children in a natural setting, believes that there is one model that, used properly, will "explain" all children. He or she will know that many models are necessary if you wish to use a model at all. The only useful model for a child, you will be told if you ask, *is* a child.

Similarly, the more experienced an ethologist is, the less use he or she will have for a concept of animals as entities whose behavior is determined by rigid, controlling instincts. The instinct model of animals breaks down when they are sufficiently observed in natural settings. If you want to know how children feel and behave, by and large do not go to a teacher of child psychology—go to a nursery school teacher. If you want to know how animals behave, do not by and large, go to an animal psychologist—go to an ethologist.

In Voltaire's words, "History is only a pack of tricks we play on the dead." It is important to step back sometimes and ask ourselves whether the way psychotherapists describe their patients, fitting them into models whether or not they belong there, seeing them only through the eyes and lenses of a particular metaphor, is not a pack of tricks they play on the living. We can do the dead no harm.

And it is not that psychologists have not been repeatedly warned of the dangers and uselessness of making models of human beings and then explaining everything in terms of these models. As J. Mck. Cattell said in an 1895 Presidential Address to the American Psychological Association:

We are past the time for simple explanations and systems, for metaphysics which explain everything in one way. The physiologist Ludwig in the 1880s wrote a classic textbook PHYSIOLOGY which explained everything on one basis—mechanism. Later he was asked why he did not prepare a new edition of it. He said "Such a work must be written by a young man; an old man is too well aware of his ignorance."[4]

Gordon Allport, one of the few modern psychologists who comprehended that psychology needed a method of science adapted to human beings, wrote:

A colleague, a good friend of mine, recently challenged me to name a single psychological problem not referable to rats for its solution. Considerably startled, I murmured something, I think, about the psychology of reading disability. But to my mind came flooding the historic problems of the aesthetic, humorous, religious, and cultural behavior of men. I thought how men build clavichords and cathedrals, how they write books, and how they laugh uproariously at Mickey Mouse; how they plan their lives five, ten, or twenty years ahead; how, by an elaborate metaphysic of their own contrivance, they deny the utility of their own experience, including the utility of the metaphysic that led them to this denial. I thought of poetry and puns, of propaganda and revolution, of stock markets and suicide, and of man's despairing hopes. And of the elementary fact that human problem-solving, unlike that of the rat, is saturated through and through with verbal function, so that we have no way of knowing whether the delay, the volition, the symbolizing and categorizing typical of human learning are even faintly adumbrated by findings in animal learning.[5]

One anthropologist, A. D. W. Malefist, put it:

Skinner has appropriately selected his subjects from pigeons and rats who can make only direct responses to stimuli. In order for man to be conditioned and manipulated in similar ways, it would be necessary to reduce him to a status similar to those captive animals and reduce him to the precultural, presymbolic and pre-creative level of existence.[6]

From the anthropologist's viewpoint, animals and humans learn and respond in very different *kinds of ways.* Animals do not have symbolic speech and can only learn from immediate experience. No animal could conceive of a concept such as "We are of such stuff/As dreams are made on . . ." or "Glory be to God for dappled things." Or, in the words of the philosopher and semanticist Alfred Korzybski, "When a symbolic class of life enters the arena, hold your hats. All bets are off."[7]

The influence of unverbalized concepts from the sourcebook of nineteenth-century physics was so strong that we persisted despite such warnings. After all, consider how successful the physicists were with their model of the atom as a small solar system and the electron as a particle or a wave. We ignore the fact that every modern physicist knows that an atom does *not* function as a small solar system and knows that an electron is neither a particle nor a wave. (An electron is a set of numbers, and *any model that uses characteristics from the worlds of sense is wrong and makes advances in understanding more difficult.*) Unspoken assumptions are stronger than spoken ones and are not changed by advances in understanding.

The influence of the model we use on our conceptualizations and on the way we think about and solve problems is difficult to overestimate. Think of the gorgeous arrogance of writing a book titled *The Behavior of Organisms,* which title encompasses every animal from protozoa to humans, after studying rats in highly artificial situations for ten years. Then, after fifteen more years of experiments, this time covering pigeons as well as rats, writing a book called *Science and Human Behavior.* This is indeed the "All animals are equal" dogma with a vengeance. To Skinner, "Man is merely a rat or pigeon writ large." He uses experiments with these animals to deal with such human activities as utopia planning, education for social reform, and understanding superstition. The mind boggles at this—or would if there were such a thing as mind. (And do you doubt that *yours* exists?)

Very few rats or pigeons have learned to march in military formations, establish and cheat on income taxes, turn the design of female plumage and decoration over to males who prefer other males as sexual partners, or any other of the common behaviors of the human race. Nor have they learned to establish a Red Cross for disaster relief, to compose the Fifth Symphony, or to paint *Christina's World.*

When the American psychologist went hunting animal behavior, he found one animal—the albino rat. It was a boojum—the psychologist vanished softly and suddenly. In the two major journals, *The Journal of Animal Behavior* and *The Journal of Comparative and Physiological Behavior,* the more articles that were published, the fewer species they covered.[8] As we published more and more in this field, it was literally about less and less. The end of the story is well known. Edwin Chase Tolman dedicated his book *Purposive Behavior in Animals and Man* to the white rat.

It has been the rat who has become the Pied Piper, leading the psychologists away from their homes, away from their concern with meaningful aspects of human life.[9]

In 1950 the psychologist Frank Beach surveyed the prestigious *Journal of Comparative and Physiological Psychology* and its forebears back to 1911.[10] He concluded that a rather stable pattern had emerged, and that psychology, as represented in this journal, had become the science of rat learning. A survey of this journal by psychologist Charles Kutscher showed that the rat, representing less than .001 percent of all living creatures, was used in 58 percent of reported studies. The rest of the studies used primates (11 percent), cats (5.1 percent), humans (9 percent), and birds (5 percent). Other species reports were less than 1 percent each.[11]

The essential reasoning behind the use of rats and pigeons is that since all behavior consists of reflexes, and since one reflex is very like another, all behavior of all species is very similar in all important aspects, and therefore we might as well use animals we can give shocks to, we do not have to pay, and whose lives we can completely control.

What is forgotten, among other things, is that each species is very different and that one generalizes at one's peril. Chickens are likely to starve to death if one inhibits their pecking for food past the developmental period when chickens naturally learn to peck. If, however, you keep swallows from flying long past the developmental period when swallows naturally learn to fly, they fly excellently at the first opportunity. This has been known for ninety years. Rats reared in darkness show no signs of impaired visual acuity when brought into light, whereas apes raised this way were functionally blind and only slowly regain visual ability. Fish are similar to apes in this regard; when raised in darkness they cannot respond to food on the basis of visual cues when moved to a lighted environment. Humans blind from birth, who later recover visual ability, respond like the apes; it takes them a considerable time to learn to use visual cues.

Which is a better model for man in terms of the importance of developmental periods, chickens or swallows? By and large psychologists have chosen chickens because this fits in with what they wanted to believe on the basis of other theories they happened to be espousing at the time. There seems to have been no other particular reason or evidence for this choice.

So strong is the influence of an unverbalized assumption—in this case, that all behavior is basically composed of the same units and therefore is basically the same and that we can study the behavior of any organism, including humans, by studying a simpler organism—that even clear and hard evidence to the contrary does not change our thinking or our behavior.

This is demonstrated in a classic paper, "The Misbehavior of Organisms" by Kellar and Marian Breland, published in the *American Psychologist* in 1961. The Brelands are two animal psychologists who had, in 1951, written a ". . . wholly affirmative and optimistic paper saying in essence that the principles derived from the laboratory could be applied to the extensive control of behavior under nonlaboratory conditions. . . ."[12] They worked with a wide variety of species, including such unusual subjects as reindeer, cockatoos, raccoons, pigs, porpoises, and whales. What they found was that when they applied the principles of operant conditioning to these exotic species (but far less exotic than humans), they ran into a persistent pattern of failure.

This is critical to the validity of the whole concept of studying animals in order to understand man. The Brelands used the most basic and established techniques and concepts from the laboratory. These techniques should have worked on the subjects if there was any validity for the study of animals in the laboratory. They didn't. The implications are clear. They were ignored.

Typical of the Brelands' work was the following procedure, which works perfectly with white rats and pigeons. The animal is trained to press a bar. It receives (from a slot below the bar) a token adapted to the species: a "penny" of a size the animal species being studied can carry easily. The animal is further trained to take the token across the cage and deposit it in another slot. The animal then receives a reward of food: an apple for a pig, some grains of corn for a chicken, and so forth. Rats and pigeons continue this behavior once they have learned it for as long as they are hungry. When they get hungry again, they start the behavior again. There is no problem here and if you are a good Behaviorist psychologist, you understand how human beings function in the same way and learn, by means of identical conditioning and reward sequences, to paint the Mona Lisa, design a space suit, and march against apartheid.

The problem the Brelands ran into, however, was that their other species could learn how to press the bar, take the token across the cage, drop it in the slot, wait for the food, and then eat it, but that after a few times in which they displayed their ability to do this sequence flawlessly, they stopped doing it and did something else. The pigs would still be very hungry, but after a few apples, they would take the large wooden pennies they were given and bring them to a corner of the cage (or enclosure they were worked in), drop them and root around them. Why did they do this? Clearly, because they were pigs, not white rats. The chickens would learn the sequence, do it a few times, and then, still hungry, take their small wooden pennies, bring them to the center of the cage, drop them and scratch around them. Why? They were chickens. That's why. Whales and porpoises would take their tokens—beach balls and inner tubes—across the pool a few times and then, still hungry, would toss them in the air and/or swallow them. And so forth up and down the range of the phylogenetic scale the Brelands explored. One might assume that human beings would learn the sequence easily and then, after a few times, would begin to pile the tokens against the wall in an attempt to climb out of the cage, try to use them as fuel to burn the walls of the cage down, play Frisbee with them, or something else at least as interesting as the use the pigs, chickens, and whales made of the tokens *they* received.

This major paper was written in a readable and humorous style. It came from an unimpeachable source. It was published in a place psychologists could not help seeing it. But it was ignored because it ran counter to the unverbalized assumption that the way to study a science was to make a model of your subject and then analyze the model. This idea works for molar physics and mechanics. It does not work for human beings.

The philosopher Ernst Cassirer has pointed out that the interpretation of myths has proved to be a magic mirror in which each school of interpreters sees only its own face or a reflection of what it wants and expects to see.[13] Thus some schools see linguistic confusions, some the movements of the sun and moon, some unconscious statements of human sexual wishes and fears, some cosmic truths, and others a wide variety of other possibilities. Similarly, a metaphor for man is also a magic mirror reflecting only the wishes and expectations of whoever makes the metaphor and then falls into the trap of believing that it reflects the subject of his study rather than a distorted caricature. The seven blind men and the elephant are a rather good metaphor for the psychologists who make metaphors for humankind.

A basic aspect of the problem for the human sciences is that, in this field, the model chosen reflects the temper of the times and the orientation of the particular scientist and has little to do with the subject itself. A "scientific" explanation of the behavior of a person tells us very little about the person, but a great deal about the viewpoint, culture, and thinking of the explainer.

Once a metaphor for man, such as the rat or the computer, is set up and used, we are in an especially tricky and dangerous situation. "For once such parallels are set up, there is no way of curbing the reader's labyrinthine associations, no clear-cut check by which to separate actual from imaginary likenesses in interpretation."[14]

One reason for the belief that humans and animals *must* be basically, qualitatively, the same lies in the history of our culture. In the attempt to dethrone the religious view of reality of the Middle Ages and replace it with the "scientific" view of the Renaissance, it was deemed necessary to get rid of the concept of the soul. If animals and humans were qualitatively the same, then either gnats and flies had souls or humans did not. The logical conclusion was obvious once the premise was accepted.

And in the present age, when the average scientist seems as terrified of finding that he has a soul as a medieval monk would have been of finding out that he did not, it is a basic of the religion of science that there is only a quantitative difference between human and animal. Otherwise, humans, if *qualitatively* different from animals, might have souls.[15]

If we look deeply, many of the assumptions of modern science, assumptions that we accept without much verbalization or thought, turn out to be remnants of an old and long-past battle to get rid of a view of reality that has long since passed out of our world.

"GOD IS AN ENGINEER"

The fifth basic concept that psychology took from the physical sciences at the turn of the century is that everything works on the same principle as a steam engine—that God is an engineer. This concept underlies nearly all the models that we have used for human beings. The idea is that, when you get right down to it, when you *really* understand how humans function (the question "What makes them tick?" reveals all too clearly the analogy to a clock), you will find that the basic principles of mechanics apply, just as they do to a machine. One might say that instead of a psychology, we have been trying to develop a physics of human behavior. And it did not work any more than a psychology of printing presses or a sociology of meteorites would work. And for the same reason.

The truth of the matter is that, work with it as hard and brilliantly as we could, this concept just did not help us comprehend or improve human consciousness or behavior. No mechanical device ever felt (or helped us understand) pity that scorches the heart, aspiration that rends the sky, anger at the oppressor, rage at injustice, love for another person—to list only a few of the feelings that make us human beings unique.

I have included here only the positive aspects of human beings—for two reasons. First, any psychology that ignores or cannot deal with these is so irrelevant and trivial that it is very difficult to understand why anyone would waste his or her time on it.

The second reason is that the mechanical theory of human beings can be used to make people worse, but cannot be used to make them better. Psychology has succeeded in one, so-called *practical* area—advertising, where it can make people more robotlike, more machinelike, but not less so.

The major goal of advertising psychology is to make people more alike, more predictable, more controllable. It is to make them march in ordered lines, all with the same motivations and tastes, to buy the same brand of canned dog food, automobile, deodorant, or cigarette. In this psychology has been successful.

We have known for a long time that the more healthy an area of human personality is, the more free and unpredictable the person is in that area. The sicker and more damaged a particular area of his personality is, the more rigid and controllable he is in that area of thought and behavior. This goes not only for areas of personality in a particular person, but for the entire person as well. The more psychological damage that has been done to him, the more we can predict his behavior. And conversely, the healthier he is psychologically, the more spontaneous and—within certain limits, that is, of being unwilling to hurt other humans—the more free and unpredictable he is.

Those involved in the advertising business strive constantly to make people more predictable, more moblike, and more controllable. In doing this, they make them less healthy. They strive to make people more antlike and less individual and free. They are among the most violent people in our society in that this striving is also a striving to make people more pathological. And it is in this work, and only in this work, that the machine model of human being is "successful," enabling those using it to achieve their ends.

The kinds of success are, of course, limited by the method and model used, but they are considerable. The advertising psychologists can make people go to war, but cannot make them strive for peace. They can make very large numbers of them buy the same toxic chemicals to put on their lawns, but are not able to make them love and cherish the environment of their only planet. They can sell them high-fat hamburgers literally by the billions, but they are unsuccessful at teaching people to care actively for their bodies, souls, and children. The use of the mechanical model can successfully be used to make human beings less, but not to make them more.

(It does not appear to be accidental that the crusading exponent of the mechanical model in psychology—John B. Watson—went into the advertising field when he left academic psychology. It is true that he left by request, but some time after leaving, he told a fellow psychologist, Arthur Jenness, that he much preferred his new profession to his old one. "In the academic world," he said, "when you have an affair with your secretary, they fire you. In business, they fire the secretary.")[1]

We see clearly how people treat each other in countries where there is an official philosophy using the mechanical model. The Soviet Union is only one example of this.

Once Isaac Newton had shown, in the late 1600s, that our understanding of the laws of mechanics could be applied not only to machines we built, but also to the working of the solar system, the next step in our thinking was inevitable. As Tennyson says in his "In Memoriam," "The stars . . . blindly run." Does this mean that molecules, mice and men also "blindly run?" This has been one of the great problems of the twentieth century and the major problem of its psychology. Mechanism is clearly a good concept for millstones, mousetraps, and other machines. Where else is it valid? Where else does it apply? Is it true for all reality? Overall, the decision in Western science was that it *did* apply to all reality.

By the 1870s, the idea that there was *anything* in the cosmos that did not fit into the mechanical model was regarded as heretical and antiscientific. In his Presidential Address to the British Association for the Advancement of Science, Thomas Henry Huxley—the most colorful and charismatic popularizer of Darwin—stated that consciousness must be automatic and subject to inexorable laws like those of mechanics, "subject to mechanical laws resembling those that govern inanimate matter."[2] The mind-computer idea was clearly stated in this talk.

We somehow had come to the amazing conclusion that when studying anthropos we cannot be anthropomorphic without losing our scientific status. It is as if astronomers came to the conclusion that in their work they could not study the night sky because astrology had done so much of that and therefore it would not be scientific to do.[3]

Arnold Toynbee called this the "apathetic fallacy." Instead of endowing everything with something like life and will and purpose (as in the "pathetic fallacy"), the living is basically dealt with as if it were nonliving, the conscious as if nonconscious.[4]

Once we were embarked on this course, it led us to strange and empty places. We studied human beings as if they had no consciousness, no "purpose," no meaning. And designing experiments and theories with this in mind, we *found* no consciousness, no purposes, no meaning. Any theory or experiment delimits in advance the *kind* of thing it will find, and ours found what we had designed our experiments to find. (The old definition of science as a series of jumps from unwarranted assumptions to foregone conclusions may not be inappropriate here.) The outcome of our basic assumption that human beings work on the same principles as machines can be illustrated by a quotation from a book by one of the apostles of this theory, B. F. Skinner (it is not parody. It is as hard to parody Skinner as it was Eisenhower):

> *The verbal stimulus "come to dinner" is an occasion on which going to a table and sitting down is usually associated with food. The stimulus comes to be effective in in-*

creasing the probability of that behavior and is produced by the speaker because it does so.[5]

The human being has vanished. A strange set of robots interact here in a nightmare world. Imagine waking up one day and finding yourself in it.

This concept—that because machines have no consciousness, then human beings do not either (or, at the very least, must be treated as if they do not)—runs all through the field; it is not the prerogative of a simple few extremists. Let us look at the utterances of a few outstanding figures of psychology. (I shall leave out the Watsons and Skinners. It is not interesting to shoot fish in a barrel.)

A leading psychotherapist, Lawrence Kubie, writes: "Although we cannot get along without the concept of consciousness, actually there is no such thing."

A leading neurophysiologist, Karl Lashley, puts it: "The knower as an entity is an unnecessary postulate."

A leading academic psychologist, D. O. Hebb, writes: "The existence of something called consciousness is a venerable *hypothesis*, not a datum, not directly observable. . . ."[6]

After pointing out how the difficulty of dealing with consciousness is eliminated by such astonishing declarations, M. Polanyi goes on to say:

> *The manifest absurdity of such a position is accepted by these distinguished men as the burden of their scientific calling. Neurologists, like all the rest of us, know the difference between consciousness and unconsciousness; when they deny it, they mean that, since it eludes explanation in terms of science, its existence endangers science and must be denied in the interest of science. Indeed, any neurologist who would seriously challenge this bigotry would be regarded as a nuisance to science.*[7]

This is indeed a strange, empty world. Empty of those specifically human qualities that make it possible for us to survive. (It reminds one of those eerie canvases of Giorgio de Chirico, with their alien structures and no human figures at all.) It does not contain *purpose*, that most characteristic of human attributes. No machine has purpose; it simply reacts to the stimuli that fall on it. But we all know that humans *do* have purpose. Each of us has it. No one ever tried to study his or her own behavior without the use of this concept. Indeed, the idea of doing so is ludicrous.

Further, it condemns us to live in the kind of space and time that machines live in, not in the special blends of feeling and memory, of hope and fear, of love and noncaring that make up the space-time synthesis that *we* can exist in. As Gordon Allport put it:

> *What nonpersonalistic psychology is able, for example, to give an intelligible setting to the fact that my seat mate in the plane is distant from me while the friend toward whom I am riding is already near to me? The essence of space and time, psychologically considered, is their* personal *relevance. Events are distant when they lack such relevance; near when they possess it. The synthesis of space and time is likewise possible on the basis of personalistic theory, for there is at the center of my experience the feeling of* here-and-now, *an unanalyzable blend of space-time.*[8]

No machine could ever describe the time element of this in the way the poet Rainer Maria Rilke did:

> *Wishes are memories that come from the future. . . . To some extent the future is already in the present. What we call the future works in exactly the same way as what we call the past. Both of them, united within us, form the complete present.*[9]

Not only could a machine not produce this description, the description itself would not be true or valid for the world in which the machine exists. It *is* true and valid for humans.

An inexorable development of the basic assumption that the laws of mechanics cover all realms of experience—make up all of reality—is the newest official psychiatric classification manual of the American Psychiatric Association, known as the *DSM-3*—the Diagnostic and Statistical Manual III. This is a very useful classification system of psychiatric problems from the viewpoint of computer storage and retrieval; it lists psychiatric problems in a manner ideal to entering them in a computer. On the other hand, it seems to have remarkably little to do with human feelings, consciousness, or behavior.

One can clearly see the next development coming down the pike—the ability to describe in advance how long each disease syndrome will take to treat. The obvious reasoning is that if the syndromes are such discrete and clear entities as the *DSM-3* says they are, they should all be treatable in the same way and in the same amount of time. We can specify how long it will take to treat syndrome number 307.60. The insurance companies will then specify how many treatments each case of 307.60 will require in office visits and/or hospital days. Thus, when a case is diagnosed, the treating physician will know in advance exactly how much he will be paid. It will simplify bookkeeping considerably. If a specific patient requires longer treatment than the specs indicate, there will be two choices. Either he will not get adequate care, or the physician will not get paid for his extra work. In terms of their previous experience with the medical profession, I leave it to each reader to guess whether the patient or the physician will be shortchanged.

(Six months after writing the previous paragraph, I have found out that the prediction is now coming true. Insurance companies are doing exactly as predicted above. To the minds of those who design modern medical payment systems, there seems to be little difference between the following two payment-rate schedules:

■ 1983 Buick Skylark, right front fender badly dented—$175.00
■ Fifty-year-old male, chronic anxiety—$200.00)

Next, of course, will be statements of the one correct method
to treat each of the syndromes described in the *DSM-3*—so
many psychotherapy sessions of such and such a type, so many
grains of such and such a medication per day, and so on. And
God help the physician who does not follow this exactly—he
will be completely vulnerable to malpractice suits. This is the
system used in ancient Egypt. Each syndrome was precisely described and the correct and approved procedures described. Under penalty, the physician had to follow the approved treatment
procedure. If, however, it did not work in four days, the physician could use any other procedure he felt indicated. I wonder
if *our* next step will include a similar amount of judgment left
to the individual physician.

One major factor that is left out of the scientific model we took
from physics—and therefore left out of the desiccated caricature
of a human being we see through the eyes of the psychology
textbooks and courses—is the spiritual factor. Human beings
have—all through history—sacrificed peace of mind, comfort of
body, and often life itself for spiritual reasons. This is one of
the major differences between the entities studied by us and the
entities studied by those concerned with material things. It is
such an essential and prominent difference that to leave it out
in our attempts to understand human beings is the equivalent
of studying airplanes and ignoring the fact that they have wings.
     It is not only the academic psychologist who has ignored
this factor. It is also the psychotherapist. Anyone who works
in this field without a keen and continual appreciation of the
fact that man's spiritual needs are as urgent and their fulfillment
as necessary for health as are his physical and emotional needs
is doing his or her patients a vast disservice. The therapist is
pretending, and teaching his patients to pretend, that a major
part of them does not exist. Psychotherapy is a spiritual as well
as psychological discipline. Over the entrance to the office of

Carl Jung was a sign to remind both patient and himself of this. It read: AVOCATUS ATQUE NON-AVOCATUS DEUS ADERIT (whether or not he is called, the God will be present). I urge a similar viewpoint on all who are therapists or patients or both.

The major, overall premise that the social sciences took from nineteenth-century physics was that when God constructed the cosmos, He (or She, if you will) was limited to using the same principles as those used by a Victorian engineer. "Man," wrote Thomas Carlyle, "works in the same way as does a steam engine." We believed this and built it into the basic structure and principles of psychology.

This basic belief led to three, generally unverbalized, concepts that have been widely accepted in the social sciences, particularly in psychology:

■ Everything that is, including the mind, works on mechanical principles.
■ We can only really understand how something works by analyzing it into its smallest "real" parts and then learning how these parts interact with each other.
■ The scientist should not have any values in his research, but just be objective.

I. THE IDEA OF UNIVERSAL MECHANISM

The decision of psychology to accept the world view of physics as valid for its own domain was made almost inevitable, not only by the tremendous prestige of the physical sciences around 1900, but by a decision that had been taken by Western thought far earlier. A major turning point of the Western world view was made at the end of the seventeenth century, at which point a philosophical argument that had raged strongly for half a century was regarded as solved. Leibniz and Descartes believed that the body and the physical world must be "explained" in one set of terms and the mind in another. Hobbes,

following Democritus and St. Thomas Aquinas, had argued that
everything in the cosmos could and must be explained in one
way only. Impressed by Galileo's mechanical experiments, he
believed that that was the correct view and method. The palm
went to Hobbes and the future course of psychology was very
strongly influenced.

As philosopher George Santayana put it:

> We have ignored an important aspect of Descartes' un-
> derstanding and returned to the view of Democritus. De-
> mocritus believed that inexorable mechanisms lay at the
> heart of everything—the materials of nature, our bodies,
> our minds, the Gods themselves. Descartes, that it lay at
> the heart of material things only.[10]

The attraction of the mechanical model should not be underestimated. Even Leibniz nearly succumbed to it—and was aware
of this. He wrote: "Their fine ways of explaining nature me-
chanically charmed me." However, both he and Descartes
clearly pointed out that the body must be explained in terms
of the principles on which the body works, and the mind must
be explained in terms of the principles on which the mind
works. Hobbes, however, believed that everything, including
the human mind, could be explained in the same way.

The very presence of the machine, everywhere and always
at hand, taught those of us in the Western world to see through
the eyes of mechanical science and to view the world through
the principles of mechanics. In social philosopher Lewis Mumford's words:

> A surviving primitive might, here and there, vent his anger
> on a cart that got stuck in the mud by breaking up its
> wheels, in the same fashion that he would beat a donkey
> that refused to move; but the mass of mankind learned
> . . . that certain parts of the environment can neither be
> intimidated nor cajoled. To control them one must learn
> the laws of their behavior.[11]

J. S. Mill stated the viewpoint clearly in his *System of Logic* in 1843:

> *The backward state of the moral [psychological] sciences can only be remedied by applying to them the methods of the physical sciences, duly expanded and generalized.*

Auguste Comte and others agreed with Mill on what psychology should be like when it would come into existence. They defined in advance of the data what they would find and how it should be studied. This is a cardinal error in all science.

Sometimes, the most excellent-sounding advice, like that given by Mill, is deadly to follow. Brutus's superb speech in *Julius Caesar* ("There is a tide in the affairs of men . . .") showed why going to battle immediately was wise; the battle that followed led to his defeat and death. Further, the historian and philosopher Friedrich Hayek has warned us: "Never will man penetrate more deeply into error than when he is continuing on a road which has led him to great success."

We have followed Mill's advice and have found that he led us into a swamp. When we started we had very little data and only theories we knew were long outmoded. Today we have mountains of data (most of it trivial in nature) and many theories all disagreeing with each other, root and branch. As Sigmund Koch said:

> It is rare that an experiment claimed to support a given theory is seen in that light by advocates of an alternate theory; it is rarer still that an experiment "generated" by a given theory, or merely performed in its ambiance, is seen by the outgroup as defining a non-trivial or valid empirical relationship.[12]

The attempt to apply the mechanical theory to human beings never did work, and in our hearts, we knew that it never could. We knew that we ourselves did not work on the same principles as a steam engine and that we had better be pretty careful as to whom and when we applied it to others. It might be possible to apply it to a "them," but never to a "thou." One is reminded here of the physicist Arthur Eddington's charming statement about the scientist who

> . . . *is convinced that all phenomena arise from electrons and quanta and the like [and who] must presumably hold the belief that his wife is a rather elaborate differential equation; but is probably tactful enough not to obtrude this opinion in domestic life.*[13]

The essence of Galileo's revolution, which started modern science on its path, was that he kept pointing to how things happen. His predecessors and opponents kept trying to deal with *why* they happen. This was the crucial shift from Final Causes (why) to Efficient Causes (how). It made modern physical science possible.

The problem that arose for us is that people—the subject matter of psychology—operate in important matters from Final Causes (why). I go down the street to buy a newspaper. That is my Final Cause. It is *why* I go down the street. To study my going down the street without including my goal is arrant nonsense. A car goes down the street because of the interaction of its parts and the road. This is the *how* (Efficient) Cause. The car has no *goal*, no Final Cause. To study *why* it goes down the street, its *purpose*, is nonsense. Galileo was right for his material, wrong for ours. However, we were so impressed by the success of the Galilean revolution that we sacrificed our duty and right to be empirical, to look at what is without preconceptions. We took to the method appropriate to Galileo's material, not to our own, thereby emulating and outdoing Esau, the biblical figure who sold his birthright for a mess of pottage.

One description of the necessity for the inclusion of causality in human life was made by Søren Kierkegaard: "We live forward and think backward"!

Early in this century the influential animal psychologist

Lloyd Morgan introduced into animal psychology a law that became widely accepted and became known as "Lloyd Morgan's Canon":

> In no case may we interpret an action as the outcome of a higher physical faculty if it can be interpreted as the outcome of the exercise of one which stands lower in the psychological scale.

However well this keeps us from interpreting the behavior of white rats as due to deep philosophical principles to which the rats are committed, it is useless for interpreting molar (large-scale, meaningful) behavior of human beings and leads us into traps such as that of the individual psychologist who tells us that he has carefully thought the matter through and that there is no such thing as thought, only conditioning, and believes that, after this intellectual suicide, we should take him seriously.

The philosopher Morris Raphael Cohen wrote, "If you deny that things are what they are, you annihilate all reason, all sanity and discourse."[14] This is what psychology has done in denying the basic reality of "what is," our goals, our feelings, our hopes, fears, joys, and sorrows. Instead of looking within and accepting our *life*, we have made these things into something else entirely—into reflexes, conditionings, complexes, and God only knows what else. In the words of the poet Novalis, "The mysterious path lies inward."

"Physics," said Santayana, "cannot account for human affairs. . . . All of our proofs are, as they say in Spain, pure conversation." We must, if we wish to make real progress, adapt our science to our data, not vice versa as we have been doing. The basic material and problems, what we can do and cannot do, how we must work, are far different in psychology and in physics. For example, we can differentiate structure and function in a machine because we can study the machine either in motion or at rest. We can therefore see how function depends on structure. However, any study of mind is a study of activities. We cannot even imagine a mind absolutely at rest. Even if it existed, there would be no way to perceive or study it.[15]

Further, the necessary language is different in the two realms of experience. In spite of vast efforts, we have found that we cannot use the same language for both without risking terrible confusion. In 1666, Leibniz recorded his adolescent dream of a universal scientific language. From time to time we tried to make his dream come true. Our last and greatest attempt (and failure) can be found in *The International Encyclopaedia of Unified Science* published in the 1940s and 1950s. It couldn't be done. The "thoughts of youth are long long thoughts" but they are not yardstick long or clock time long. We need different languages for different realms. Galaxies, tops, and electrons all have "spin" (and so does my mind when I consider the problem), but the term means something very different in each case. The "energies" in an electrical battery, a painting by Picasso, an angry crowd, and my hopes for the future are entirely different kinds of meanings and terms. The same word, used in different realms of experience, means something entirely different.

Seymour Sarason, with his wide experience and erudition, has pointed out in detail the widespread negative influence of the mechanical approach and the machine model in psychology. He ends by noting that, "Indeed, after World War II the social sciences seemed far more interested in the history of the physical sciences than in that of their own fields." Sarason documents the degree to which we have lost contact with our subject matter and, in the course of this, have almost completely neglected the study of ourselves as psychologists, as members of our society, and the study of the influence that cultural changes have on us.[16]

Sarason's view can be demonstrated by his writing on the way that psychologists (and geneticists also, but that is not *our* problem) change their opinion of data to fit the social climate. Before 1930, different human races were believed, on the basis of "scientific evidence," to be different in intelligence. After 1940, the reverse was true. There was not that much new information. We simply "found out" that it meant something else as the climate of opinion changed.

And woe to the psychologist who did not change fast enough. Like the citizen of a communist country who has not kept up with changes in political dogma, the psychologist who lags behind is likely to find himself in trouble. His University Tenured Position is suddenly far less secure than he believed. The strong guard of individual opinion turns out to be a weak reed indeed. (As evidence of the strength of this, I find myself impelled to point out that I am not saying anything here about the average intelligence level of different races, I am speaking about the behavior of psychologists.)

There is also a new wave developing in psychology; a major change is beginning to take place. New articles and books are appearing pleading with us to return to a *human* science, one in which the psychologists themselves are seen as influenced by their society and as a strong influence on their subjects.

Typical of the growing reaction to the physicalist model in psychology is a recent book by David Berg and Kenwyn Smith, *Exploring Clinical Methods for Social Research.*[17] This book is based on three "firmly held beliefs":

■ The nature and findings of social science research are powerfully influenced by the relationship between the researcher and researched.
■ This aspect should be studied as intensely as any other aspect of the research.
■ Any system of investigating social reality must address the whole research process as well as the research relationship.

Berg and Smith go on to point out that in the study of elementary chemistry, standard pressure and temperature are assumed unless otherwise reported.

Thus we discover that water does not always boil at 212°
when we try to cook an egg in Denver. . . . One can

*scarcely imagine the confusion if this relationship were al-
tered and not reported. In the social sciences, however, it
is very difficult to imagine a standard relationship between
the researcher and researched.*[18]

This work almost seems to be a response to much of the Sarason
material reported earlier in this book. Repeating many of the
same type of observations he made (such as that psychologists
seem to consider themselves outside of the mainstream of their
culture when, in fact, they are very strongly influenced by it),
Berg and Smith go on to explore the problem from many angles. Theirs is an important work that has not received the
attention it deserves. This is only partly due to the fact that
the title is unclear and is not likely to attract the readers who
would be interested; it is also due to the fact that psychologists
generally are very resistant to criticisms of their basic approach
and to evaluation of the philosophy that underlies their work.
To quote William James again, "No priesthood ever initiated
it own reform."

In an interesting chapter in Berg and Smith, the psychologist Clayton Alderfer discusses the fact that the areas of the
effect of the researcher on the research and of his professional
organizations on the researcher are avoided to a very marked
degree by psychologists. As scientists, says Alderfer, we study
other people and other people's organizations.[19]

II. THE IDEA OF ANALYSIS

Another part of the nineteenth-century model for all sciences is the concept that the real way to advance knowledge is
to analyze your subject into parts, study how those parts interact, and then put them back together again. This, of course,
works very well for entities like steam engines; the engine may
even work better after you do this if you have cleaned the parts
in the process. The concept does not work very well with living
systems such as human beings, who may simply refuse to go on

functioning after you put them back together; it does not work at all when applied to consciousness, which has no "parts" into which it is divisible. There are things that break apart into sections and things that do not. The idea of a half of a book makes sense; *half* of an idea of a book does not (as the psychologist Boris Sidis pointed out long years ago). When you attempt to break the inner life—which controls our behavior—into parts, you get ridiculous results. E. B. Titchener, who brought experimental psychology to the United States, developed a school called "Structuralism" which tried it and obtained such boring meaninglessnesses that it was abandoned with a large collective yawn. Behaviorism tried it. The result was a system that, in the words of the philosopher C. D. Broad, was "so innately silly that it could only have been devised by very learned men."

Reductionism is always true, but also false. It is true, in the famous phrase, that "a Beethoven violin sonata is *nothing but* a cat's intestines scraped by a horse's tail"—true, but far more false. It is certainly not a "scientific" statement. Similarly, to regard human behavior as *nothing but* chains of reflexes, or as unconscious forces interacting with ego defenses, or some such limited aspect of behavior, is far more false than true. It is also unscientific, and, for purposes of advancing understanding, about as useful as the above explanation of a Beethoven violin solo.

And we can learn just about as much about human behavior from studies of chains of conditioned responses as we can learn about Beethoven's music from studies of the anatomy of cats and horses.

Karl Lashley, the greatest of our brain physiologists, did a thirty-year study trying to understand and explain learning in Behavioristic terms. He broke learning into parts, then tried to analyze the interaction of the parts and then put them together again. His summary, written in despair, was, "The only conclusion I can reach, on reviewing the evidence, is that learning is just not possible."[20] I can break up my behavior into the contractions of muscle groups and so forth, but this will not give me any real understanding of behavior.

In the words of the psychiatrist and theoretician Andreas Angyal:

> *Scientists have found out that the ears are for hearing, the eyes for seeing, the lungs for breathing, the hands for grasping, the feet for walking; they should now take just a step further and find out what the whole man is for. The problem stated in this way is a philosophic one; but if we formulate the problem in a somewhat different way and ask: What is the general trend in the total dynamism of the organism? What is the direction in which the total life process evolves? What is the organism aiming at in its total function?—then we have a legitimate scientific problem, which a theory of the total organism should answer.[21]*

From his work with thousands of brain-damaged soldiers, during and after World War I, Kurt Goldstein, who coined the term *self-actualization* and was a major influence on Abraham Maslow, found that it was impossible to understand their problems or to work toward solutions from the atomistic viewpoint. Only by dealing with his patients as total, indivisible persons, interacting with their environment, could he make progress.

Further, he found that the methods of natural science in which he had been so well trained were useless when working with his patients. No two were identical; no exact predictability could be found. Each was a unique case who could help him learn about how human beings with and without central nervous system damage respond to the varying situations they face. He could learn, and learn how to learn, and how to help, but he could not make general laws. Goldstein wrote

> *My greatest problem grew out of my awareness at this period that I could not achieve my goals with the methods of the natural sciences.[22]*

The historian R. G. Collingwood has pointed out that *Paradise Lost* might be just a collection of words chosen from the dictionary by Milton. We know that it is not and that each part is organically and strongly related to all the others by reading it as a whole. Similarly, a human being is not just a collection of parts but is primarily a whole. Only in *this* way do the parts make sense.

I once knew a man who learned English in his twenties. In his forties he decided that he had never read Shakespeare in the original and now wanted to. He then spent the next four years with a list of all the words in Shakespeare's plays, making sure he understood the dictionary meaning of every single word. After that he said, "Now I am ready to read Shakespeare." He was surprised to find the plays flat, insipid, lacking in any real meaning or vitality for him. The method of analysis and atomism does not work much better for reading Shakespeare than it does for studying man in the psychology laboratories. Doing so takes all the life and *meaning* out of what you are studying. This is a major reason for the growing pessimism and skepticism among psychologists that I referred to earlier.

III. THE IDEA OF OBJECTIVITY

Another piece of the model we borrowed from nineteenth-century mechanics was the idea that we can only advance our learning about something if we study it objectively and without making value judgments. There are, however, fields of science that have made real progress in which this concept is not accepted as true.

In ethology it has been found that, in Konrad Lorenz's words, you must "love" the animal you are working with.

> *It takes a very long period of watching to become really familiar with an animal and to attain a deeper understanding of its behavior; and without the love for the animal itself, no observer however patient could ever look at it long enough to make valuable observations on its behavior.*[23]

As another leading ethologist, Frank Darling, put it, you must be "intimate" with your subject. Imagine sending to a typical psychology journal (*The Journal of Experimental Psychology* and *The Psychological Bulletin* come to mind) an article that included a statement that you "loved" your subjects or were "intimate" with them. The article would bounce so fast it would not even be marked "Rejected. The Editor." Rather it would come back stamped "Opened by Mistake! The Editor."

In history today there is the basic concept that to understand what a particular period was all about, a mere compilation of the facts is not enough—not the facts of dates and battles and decisions. Instead we must, in Collingwood's words, "Think their thoughts, feel their feelings." Caesar was killed on the floor of the Senate house. We know where and when. But if we are modern historians we also need to feel what Brutus and Cassius felt, to understand what they thought they were doing. Only then can we understand. To quote Collingwood:

> To the historian, the activities whose history he is studying are not spectacles to be watched, but experiences to be lived through in his own mind. They are objective, or known to him, only because they are also subjective, or activities of his own.[24]

And if we wish to comprehend the actions of a child, we must, as Eda LeShan, a noted professional colleague of mine, has so cogently pointed out, remember the child within ourselves. Those who do not remember themselves as children in a similar situation cannot really comprehend how a child feels. We have certainly learned this in psychotherapy. Only with the empathy that comes from self-understanding and self-exploration can we comprehend our clients. (This, by the by, is one of the reasons that having had a long, serious, period of psychotherapy themselves is one of the criteria by means of which we distinguish the true psychotherapists from the charlatans.)

Further, our experience in psychotherapy has taught us that maintaining an *objective* attitude is not conducive to the patient's progress. We must *care* about the patient, we must be deeply and emotionally concerned about the best for him, for positive results to be likely. The new definition of *counter-transference* (originally given by Rollo May) is that it is "the ability to *enthusiastically* affirm the patient's growth and development."

In those areas of the study of consciousness and behavior in which we have made real progress in understanding and helping our strange and suffering species—psychotherapy, history, child development, ethology—we have found that we cannot progress without empathy, love, and personal involvement with our subject. (These of course are not enough by themselves; they are necessary but not sufficient causes, as the logicians would say. Training, long and hard, and discipline are also needed.)

A basic tenet of psychotherapy has long been that moral values have no place in the process; nothing is morally "right" or morally "wrong." But the idea of "no judgmentalism" was equated with that of "no ethical values," and few recognized that this is in itself a value system. As Rollo May put it, "The lack of value judgments which the older therapy opted for is based on a definite philosophical system—that of a fairly complete relativism."

In his usual succinct manner, Gardner Murphy, universally recognized in the profession as one of our most valuable and outstanding psychologists, has summed up both the older approach and his view of it.

> The dogmatic rationalism first uttered by Thomas Huxley, later echoed by Bertrand Russell, announced that for an enlightened, modern person, ethics is clearly a local artifact of special conditions of society, and that man can count on no cosmic support whatever for any ethical goals with which he wishes to concern himself. These confident expressions are all interesting, if quaint, responses to the empirical and

practical difficulties of determining where we are, where we are going, and what we are.[25]

If psychotherapists have begun to realize everything is judged to be relative (to the culture, to the social class, to the family, and so on), then therapists are saying in effect: "If you want a system of behavior, look around you and take the most convenient—that is, the most common." If value judgments are not openly made by therapists, the patient is likely to accept the superficial mores of this culture.

It is, of course, not possible completely to keep ethical values out of therapy. As the psychiatrist Thomas Szasz says:

> . . . it does make a difference—arguments to the contrary notwithstanding—what the psychiatrist's socioethical orientations happen to be, for these will influence his ideas on what is wrong with the patient, what deserves comment or interpretation, in what possible directions change might be possible, and so forth. . . . Can anyone really believe that a psychotherapist's ideas concerning religious beliefs, slavery, or other similar issues, play no role in his practical work? . . .[26]

While it is not possible to keep values out of therapy, it *has* been possible to try to convince the patient that the therapy was "above" values or ethical judgments. "An amoral psychotherapy," as psychologist Goodwin Watson pointed out in a classic paper, "is a contradiction in terms."[27]

Psychologist George Turner, discussing this relativity of values, indicates that because the Freudian superego is culturally defined and limited, it does not necessarily follow that all values are: "Without challenging the reality of the Freudian conscience, one can deny it exclusive rights to the territory." As a possible example, he gives the existentialist concept of *ontological guilt*, an apparently culture-free form of guilt that arises from forfeiting one's potentialities.[28]

Rollo May, after suggesting a redefinition of objectivity for the therapist ("Objectivity is the capacity to affirm the growth and development of the other person"), gives some examples of value judgments possible in therapy. These include the concept that it is better for a human being to have the ability to use his capacities and potentials, to be free and to love, than it is for him not to do these things. Further, that in interpersonal relationships, one should so act as to encourage and aid these developments in others.[29]

A general movement toward the acceptance of values in therapy appears to be in progress. There seems to be a growing feeling that being "free" of moral judgments leads to loss of self-respect, identity, and self-image. Acceptance of the idea that all the patient's undesirable behavior is due to the sins of the parents appears to weaken concepts of will, responsibility, self-control. A New Yorker cartoon showed two juvenile delinquents awaiting their appearance in court. The older one was advising the younger: "You can get off easy. Just tell them your mother hated you."

This perhaps brings up another reason for the open acceptance of ethical values in therapy. Only then is it possible for the patient to distinguish between neurotic guilt and real guilt.

PSYCHOLOGY AND THE HUMAN CONDITION

One day in the late 1960s I was in my office talking with a patient. He and I had started working two years earlier. At that time he had had very extensive cancer of both lungs. It was inoperable, and the amount of radiation needed to have done any good would have killed him by itself. He was on an experimental chemotherapy program that was later abandoned because of poor results. Now his cancer had regressed until it was hardly visible on X ray.* He said to me, "You know, Larry, the first year and a half we worked together we were never alone in this office."

I was startled and must have looked it because he went on: "I was sitting in this chair and you were in that one and in the corner over there was a man with a long beard and a scythe!" As I realized that I too had had that feeling as we had talked about living and dying, about my patients' feelings about dying and about the meaning of his life, I began to wonder how

---

*His cancer continued to regress until there were no signs of it. For two years he was disease free. He then developed a blood disease, *Polycythemia vera*, and died of it.

I, an experimental psychologist, had come to this situation. It was a long way from my courses in statistics and experimental methodology, from my early experiments in the learning of motor skills and the design of rat mazes. It was even a far cry from my training in psychoanalytic psychotherapy.

My views of the nature of life and the problems of my profession of psychology have come a long way. So far in this book, I have concentrated on what is *wrong* with psychology, both academic and clinical, today. There is, however, another side. Since the late nineteenth century, there have been those who were involved in inventing a specific method designed for the study of human beings, a scientific method applicable not to inanimate things but to we makers of art, literature, and concentration camps, we who love, kill, and succor each other. I did not know of this development at the time I was forced, by the nature of the research project on which I was working, to change my own viewpoint; I only came to learn of it, and from it, later. I will write of it and the men and women who made it, in Chapters 9 and 10, but first, here, as a typical psychologist of my time, I will describe the events that forced me to change and to begin to search beyond my own training.

In a very real sense, this book started in 1952. I had at that time a master's degree in psychology and had completed all the coursework for the Ph.D. In addition, I had worked as a clinical psychologist in the Army and in the Veterans Administration. In all of these experiences, I had worked with excellent teachers. Now, equipped with training in research methodology and in clinical psychology, I approached a major research project.

The further I worked my way into the new project, the more obvious it became that my training and experience were not applicable to it and that they had in no way prepared me for the kind of observations I was making. I was working with human adults under great stress, and the research methods I had so painfully learned were useful only to a very limited extent. Further, the theoretical viewpoint I had been taught about how human beings functioned simply was not adequate and could not accommodate the data I was accumulating. I seemed to have a limited number of choices: I had either to give up the project, to run away from the data and take refuge in theories about what I *should* have been finding, or to get out of the field of psychology completely. The only other alternative I could see was to try to change myself, to *grow* enough to be able to develop my methods and theoretical concepts so that they would be able to include and "explain" what I was observing. This task has occupied me for more than thirty years.

The project had originally been suggested by my friend, Dr. Richard Worthington. Dick is a genius in (among other things) the interpretation of projective-test protocols. One day in 1949, he remarked to me that he had just gone over personality test material for three people who had cancer, and he felt, on the basis of what he had seen, that there was something important that we ought to know about the emotional life history of people with cancer. He went on to say that the area badly needed research.

I had learned sometime before that when Dick said something like this, it was not to be dismissed lightly. I tucked the memory away for the future.

Two years later, I was back in the Army, working as a commissioned clinical psychologist in a mental hygiene clinic in Arkansas. I remembered what Dick Worthington had said about cancer and emotional life history. There was an excellent medical library in the town of Fort Smith; in the middle of the last century, the local physicians had formed an association to which each member willed his books. I began spending my evenings there, trying to learn what I could. Looking at the cancer mortality statistics with a psychologist's eye, it was clear to me that they indicated the strong likelihood that emotional factors played a part in their variations. For example, the fact that there were lower cancer mortality rates during wartime and high peaks during the immediate postwar period seemed to suggest that what was going on in the society and how people felt about the meaning of their lives played a part in the statistics. (My first thought when I saw the differences between wartime and postwar cancer mortality statistics was that they were due to the fact that many pathologists got drafted and that there were therefore fewer autopsies done during wartime! However, examining the differential rates of external and internal cancer showed that this was not the crucial factor. If it had been, then the rate of internal cancers, harder to diagnose and needing autopsies to be certain very often, would have dropped more than external cancers, which did not require autopsies for diagnosis. This, however, was not the case.) Other statistics also indicated that I was on a potentially fruitful track. The widely known fact that the death of a spouse made the survivor more vulnerable to cancer (statistically speaking) was only one example of what I found.

When I left the Army in 1952, I showed Dick Worthington what I had found. He and I agreed that it was important that the research proceed. He called together a group of businessmen he knew; we showed them the statistics I had found, made a pitch, and before the meeting was over had raised enough money so that I could work on it half-time for a year. For the next twelve years, with the help of the Ayer Foundation, I worked full-time at the project.

Since I had the financial backing I needed and enough hospital experience to ensure that I could walk through a ward without knocking over all the bedpans, I anticipated no trouble as I confidently approached the major hospitals in New York City. To my surprise, in the first fifteen I visited, as soon as I told the research committee or the chief of Oncology or the head of Psychiatry what I wanted to do—*to see if it was fruitful to approach cancer from the viewpoint of modern psychosomatic knowledge*—I was immediately and firmly shown out of the hospital. Sometimes this was very quick. In New York's famous Memorial Hospital, one of the world's great cancer centers, I think I lasted about fifteen minutes!

A few years later I published my first paper discussing the special problems of doing psychotherapy with cancer patients and the methods I was using to work past these problems. Because she had contributed so much to my ideas on this, Dr.

Marthe Gassmann received joint credit. She was on the staff of New York's Lenox Hill Hospital at that time. Her colleagues who saw the paper in *The American Journal of Psychotherapy* were outraged. They told her it was "obscene" to devote psychotherapy time to cancer patients, when it should be devoted to people who would have a long life ahead of them in which to enjoy the benefits they received! (There were at that time very few therapists to whom I could refer patients—and as soon as the grapevine found out I was working with this type of patient, a great many people with cancer came to me for psychotherapy. Usually I had no one to whom I could send them. With a very few exceptions, such as Dr. Gotthard Booth, most trained psychotherapists were very opposed to this kind of work. The situation is completely different today.)

Until this happened, it had not occurred to me that there were still taboo subjects in science. I knew well how there had been such subjects in the past; I knew stories such as that of the physician Ignaz Semmelweiss, who was thrown out of his hospital and teaching position when he tried to get physicians to wash their hands before they worked with a woman in childbirth. Although these and other similar stories are taught to every student in science, I believed that these problems existed only in the past, not in the present. I am wiser now.

Presently, however, I was able to come to a very good working arrangement with Emmanuel Revici of the Institute of Applied Biology in New York City. After hearing what I wanted to do, he said, "We know there are unknown factors in cancer. Often a patient dies who we think, on the basis of experience and knowledge, should live, and vice versa. It may be that some of these factors lie in the area you wish to explore. Further, I have been called a charlatan so often that I won't call you one until you prove you are."

Today, with all the talk of "the immune system," when the relationship between stress and disease has been so widely explored and we even have a new word for what was then called "psychosomatic medicine" (we now call it, God save the mark, "psychoneuroimmunology"), it is hard to recall a time when the relationship between someone's emotional life history and his or her cancer was thought to be nonexistent.

I will not go into detail here about the long years of interviews, projective tests, and psychotherapy that I did with cancer patients and control groups; this material belongs in professional journal articles and has been presented there. What is important here is that in order really to deal with, to come to grips with, my observations, I had to move beyond the orientations and the approaches to human beings in which I had been trained, and which were the standard approaches for psychologists of my generation.

There were three areas in which I had to transcend my training. These were:

■ How one does research in psychology?
■ In what sort of frame of reference, with what general theory, one views human behavior?
■ What is the basic question that a therapist asks in psychotherapy?

I will discuss these in the following pages.

How does one do research in psychology? Basically, I had been taught, the psychologist identifies specific factors that can be separated out from the mass of the subject's inner life and/or behavior; one quantifies (assigns numerical values to) them and then measures their presence and absence, or their amounts, against something else. One takes the presence or absence of responses to the entire Rorschach card (rather than to parts of the specific inkblot) and measures the frequency of these in subjects with a regular work history and in subjects who have changed jobs on an average more than once every two years. Or one might study the amount of satisfaction in their marital state, as measured and quantified on a paper-and-pencil questionnaire, against the subject's parents' marital history. (As a student I had perhaps done this almost to a reductio ad absurdum, to a degree that made it ridiculous, by correlating the number of times white mice vibrated their whiskers at each choice point of a maze against the correct or incorrect choice they made in the direction they took at that choice point. I forget the reason for this study, but it did seem meaningful and important at the time!) In any case, the basic thing that I had been taught about psychological research was that one took separate factors that could be quantified (or, at least, measured with a "present" and "absent") and measured them against other separate factors.

Of course, it was somewhat more complex than this: often we would measure several, or more, factors against each other. We used elaborate statistical techniques such as Factor Analysis to measure these relationships and to group them and manipulate them against each other, but the basic technique was the same.

In working with cancer patients, I had one of the two factors I needed: they either had cancer or they did not. (This did not mean the two groups were really separate; some of the "not" group could have had undiagnosed cancers, but as a single criterion, this would do.) I had one factor, a reasonably objective one. What about psychological factors I could measure against it?

At this point, I encountered a major surprise. There were many "objective" factors I could measure against the diagnosis: marital history, the childhood death of a sibling, occupational status, amount of time the subject had been the youngest child, intelligence and projective-test scores, frequency of change in living location, occupational satisfaction, and so forth. Many of these did correlate to a statistically significant degree with the diagnosis and I dutifully published these correlations in the professional journals along with the clues to further understanding that I drew from them. As a means of testing hypotheses that I had arrived at by quite other means—by means of *understanding* and comprehending the worlds my patients lived in— the techniques I had learned were useful. They were not useful, however, for discovering anything new about the people I was working with. To do that, I had first to suspect something, then check it out with these methods. I had to *choose* what I wanted to measure against the diagnosis on the basis of theory. Then I could test it.

At this time I came across the work of the great American biometrician Raymond Pearl, who showed that the statistical method was useful for testing hypotheses, but not for finding new ideas. Further—and this proved crucial—the statistics could indicate the amount of a measurable factor in large groups of subjects, but *could tell nothing of its meaning for any specific individual.* In a way, this was the essence of the problem. I never had a collection of cells come into my office any more than I had statistical groups of people come in. (The head of the British Cancer Society, Sir David Smithers, once said that cancer is no more a disease of cells than a traffic jam is a disease of automobiles. In neither case will study of the wrong thing solve the problem. You will not stop traffic jams by studying the internal combustion engine, he said, any more than you will cure cancer by studying cells. In both cases, it is a matter of a general ecology, one of a city, the other of a human being.) Unique individuals were all I saw. The fact that their total lives—biological, psychological, spiritual—included the presence of cancer at this time was a factor they all had in common.

I slowly began to understand the difference between studying groups of people and studying a person who belongs to that group. These are very different matters. For example, I can make accurate predictions regarding the group, but none regarding the individual. As I sit here in New York City, I can scientifically predict that on Friday afternoon there will be very heavy traffic on the George Washington Bridge going out of the city. But I can make no such prediction about you. *You* may decide to stay in the city and go to the theater. What I was finding out is that, although a group can be described in statistics, can have statistical predictions made about it, the experimental methods I had learned, and the ways of predicting what would happen, *applied only to groups and had nothing to do with an individual person.*

Individuals cannot be studied with the neat and precise

methods with which we analyze groups. And I was meeting individuals in my work. They had to be studied in quite a different way. I could not apply concepts and methods in an area for which they were not suited; as Freud had warned, ". . . it is dangerous, not only with men, but also with concepts, to drag them out of the region where they originated and where they have matured."[1] I needed a way of doing research that was scientific, but very different from the methods of academic psychology. I needed to combine a scientific method for studying individuals with the scientific method for studying groups.

A case in point that may illustrate this is the relationship of intelligence to one form of cancer. There is a particular cancer—Hodgkin's disease, a cancer of the lymphatic system—that tends to be found in much younger people than many others. It tends to be found mostly in the late teens, the twenties, and thirties. I had seen ten and worked intensively with five people with this diagnosis. They all impressed me as being above average in intelligence, some of them very bright indeed. Was this finding due to chance, to the kind of patients who were attracted, at that time, to the cancer center I was working in, to the fact that I cared very much about these people and tend to overestimate the intelligence of people I care about, or was there a real relationship between the diagnosis of Hodgkin's disease and intelligence? Obviously this was something to be tested statistically with the methods with which I had been trained.

I devised a method and went to Walter Reed Army Medical Center with it. They had access to a large group of men who had been given an intelligence test immediately after having been examined physically and shown no sign of the disease, and who some years later were diagnosed as having Hodgkin's disease. These were soldiers who had been given a rather good group intelligence test (the AGCT) at their induction, when they were healthy as measured by their induction physical examinations, and who later, during their years in the Army or afterward, were diagnosed either by the Army or by the Veterans Administration as having this condition. In our sample, which had only enlisted men, we had over four hundred men who if they indeed constituted a random sample of army enlisted, should have had an average AGCT score of 100. They did not. Their average score was significantly above this. Other measurements of the group confirmed this finding.

So—Hodgkin's disease is selective; it tends to be found in people who are above average in intelligence. (Incidentally, it is possible that this is true for cancer as a whole. So far as I know, this has never been tested.) But what exactly did this mean? Each person uses his or her intelligence in different ways. With one it may lead to high achievement. With another, who lives in a differently perceived universe and who feels different about himself and others, it will press the development of the person in an entirely different direction. Certainly high intelligence was not *the cause* of Hodgkin's, any more than a virus, genetic predisposition, or emotional loss was *the cause*. One cannot look at one brick in a building and say, "Aha, that is why the building stays upright," or "See that brick—it is the whole building."

I could tell some things about groups of people who had been diagnosed with cancer and how the frequency of certain factors (for example, death of a spouse) differed in this group and "similar" groups (age, social class, and so on) who did not have this diagnosis. The only factor that differentiated the two groups 100 percent of the time was the present diagnosis. (There were even Hodgkin's disease patients I later saw who were of normal or low intelligence.) But I could tell nothing about *individuals* from these "objective" measurements, and it was with individuals that I was dealing. No large groups of cancer patients came into my office, only individual and unique persons with this diagnosis. How could the knowledge that 70 percent of cancer patients (as opposed to 10 percent of equated controls) had lost a major way of relating between six months and eight years before the first diagnosis help me understand let alone help someone who came into my office with cancer of the pancreas? Even if this particular person was one of the 70 percent, how would *that* help? The facts, including the facts of our inner life, are never as important as the context they are in and how we feel about them. Indeed, to separate the facts from the context in which they are viewed by the individual himself makes them meaningless. Victor Frankl, the psychiatrist who learned so much about being human from his experiences in the German concentration camps, used to tell the following story to teach this: There were, during a bombardment in World War I, two soldiers who found themselves huddling at the bottom of a shellhole. One was a Prussian officer, the other an Austrian private. The Prussian officer asked, "Are you afraid?" The private replied, "I'm terrified." "That," said the officer, "shows the superiority of race and training. I am not frightened." "No," replied the private, "It shows the difference, not the superiority. If you were one half as frightened as I am, you would have run away long ago."

I found nothing important about the people I worked with that could (a) be separated from the whole of the person, or (b) be quantified. And yet I had been taught that to do psychological research, to be a scientist, I needed to study the relationship between factors that had these precise characteristics. Merely finding or giving a number to a "high anxiety level," says nothing of any value. What relationship does this "high" anxiety level (high according to the measurement technique you are using at the moment—which is probably the one that is "chic" and "in" in your particular field at the moment)* bear to the rest of the total person? What is meaningful is the overall *pattern* of their being, of their perceptions and reactions. I began to come to the belief that trying to understand a human being by the analytic techniques I had learned, by trying to break him down into measurable pieces, was like trying to un-

*How a psychologist measures "anxiety level" is largely a matter of fashion. I recall periods when any study that did not use the Taylor Anxiety Scale was very likely not to get published. At other times, everyone in the field was using scores from the Minnesota Multiphasic Personality Inventory. At other periods, the Rorschach Test was used. One hopes for the day when measurement instruments will be chosen according to how relevant they are to the problem, not how relevant they are to current fashion.

derstand a van Gogh painting by counting the brush strokes and determining what percentage of them slanted in each direction. That could prove an interesting exercise and could make me feel like a "scientific" art historian, but it was certainly going to bring me no nearer to understanding the painting or knowing how to respond to it.

For what was truly important and unique about each person I needed more. I needed the flavor and pattern of life. I needed objectivity *and* disciplined subjectivity. I found, rather to my dismay, that Tolstoy's magnificent description of a cancer patient in *The Death of Ivan Illyich* helped me to comprehend my patients far more than the statistical findings on cancer incidence. If I wanted to learn from the people I worked with (to say nothing of helping them), I had to comprehend their experience as well as understand it. This became clearer and clearer as I proceeded. However, it was this very subjectivity I had been repeatedly warned against in my training. A scientist, I had been taught, is objective, does not get personally involved with his material.

I felt trapped in a paradox. If I remained objective, I could only understand bits and pieces of my patients. I could not see them as the whole coherent and unique persons they were. If I both understood and empathized, I felt that I would be losing my ability to be a scientist, losing my ability to use the clear and beautiful scientific approaches I had so laboriously learned.

The patients I was seeing forced the issue. It became clear that if I wished to help them, I *must* be involved, I must care for them and about them. I could do nothing for them by maintaining a cool, detached, and objective stance, divorced from caring.

During this time I learned, in the face of my training, that a therapist cannot really help a patient grow and become unless he *cares* very much about this patient and his becoming. I had been taught that the therapist must be objective and removed from the patient. I learned now that without deep caring, little can be done. It is the therapist's caring for the patient that teaches the patient to have the kind of caring for himself that provides the nourishment for further positive development.

(Certainly I also needed to be objective and realistic. Part of the solution I found was to begin working with a control— or supervising—therapist, a highly trained psychiatrist with whom, a couple of times a week, I could go over what I was doing, how I was feeling about my patients, and how I saw them. She helped me maintain the balance between objectivity and caring, empathic involvement.)

But there is no conflict here between objectivity and subjectivity. The contradiction is far more apparent than real. Caring for a person means caring for *all* of him, the negative as well as the positive aspects. It means seeing him "warts and all" and not just viewing him in a roseate haze.

I also found that there was no conflict between the psychotherapy wherein I was involved with my patients and deeply concerned with their fates and the beautiful and elegant experimental methods in which I had been trained. It is, I believe, only when the two approaches—clinical and experimental—are combined that we are on the road to a true science of human consciousness and behavior, to a human psychology.

The second area in which I had to transcend my training in the cancer research was the question of how one does psychotherapy: What sort of approach to therapy, what general theory, was most useful?

The theoretical viewpoint I brought to this work was a straightforward psychoanalytic one. It seemed to me then that the Freudian concepts were sufficient to deal with and explain all human behavior. I had been reasonably well trained in this set of concepts in the Army and at the University of Chicago. In addition, I had had two years of modified psychoanalytic therapy (on the couch, with free association and dream interpretation—but only three times a week!). I was deeply impressed with the *completeness* of the theory, its apparent ability to explain everything humans did and felt. Also, the theory has a beauty, an elegance and a consistency, that I found very appealing.

Naturally, then, when I started on the therapy part of the research, I used a psychoanalytic frame of reference. Clearly, orthodox *procedures* were not possible with hospitalized patients in extreme physical and emotional stress, but the ideas and concepts should be. These would indicate what areas and subjects would be fruitful.

(The idea that there is such a thing as pure nondirective therapy is, of course, a myth. If a patient refers to three subjects in a discourse and you comment on or interpret one of them, you are directing the course and direction of the therapy. The therapist's ideas about what is superficial and leading somewhere else, what is central, what is worthy of interpretation, the kind of and the content of the interpretation, and so on, all indicate to the patient what the therapy is all about and where it should go in order for progress to be made. Even if the therapist remains out of the line of vision of the patient and comments only very infrequently, these things, as well as the interpretations themselves, their form and content, give strongly suggestive clues to the patient. There is no such thing as a two-person process with only one of the persons directing the course of events. Can one really believe, for example, that the therapist's attitudes on slavery, on child molestation, or even on male-female relationships do not influence the course of a therapeutic program of which he or she is a part?)

After a considerable period of trying to learn about the cancer patients who came to the Institute of Applied Biology, where I was working, I felt I had gone as far as I could with the interviews (one to eight hours with each person) and projective tests. The best way to get to really comprehend another person seemed to me to call for undertaking a psychotherapy program with them.

An immediate ethical problem arose. A psychotherapy program is designed to help someone, and any procedure strong enough to offer potential help is also strong enough to offer potential hurt. There were very few guideposts; I could find no one with extensive experience in this field, and only one study in which intensive psychotherapy with cancer patients was reported. (This 1928 study, by Elida Evans, a Jungian therapist, while helpful, was far from enough to solve the ethical problem I faced.)

Two factors made it possible for me to engage in a psychotherapy with these patients. First, every patient at the Institute received a complete biochemical workup every day, so I would have at least some clues to the effect of my work with them. The second factor was that for the first five years of the program, I only worked with "terminal" patients; that is, patients for whom the standard medical prognosis was that there was nothing to be done and they would soon die. With these two factors I felt that it was ethically legitimate for me to proceed.

My strong psychoanalytic orientation dictated the approach of the therapy. The sessions were oriented toward the past, the childhoods of the patients; dream interpretation and modified free association were used; I remained as much a blank screen as possible (in order to encourage transference to develop), and so forth. The patients were very cooperative, but over the first year and a half I became more and more uncomfortable—for three reasons.

First, there was clearly something wrong with what we were discussing. In working with a man under the hammer of fate, in a deeply critical life-stress situation with an out-of-control liver cancer, talking with him about his toilet training and sibling rivalry was clearly avoiding reality for the sake of a theory. In family therapist Nathan Ackerman's words:

> In psychoanalytic theory, present-day realities are put aside and ignored so that the transference can be built and worked through. Present-day realities are left until the patient has caught up with his childhood distortions.[2]

This was how I had been trained to work as a therapist, but it did not seem applicable here.

During this time, an incident involving Mrs. Sarah Connell, chief social worker for the Manhattan Society for Mental Health, occurred. A woman phoned her, asking for advice. She and her husband had both been in psychoanalytic therapy, he for six years, she for four. The husband's analyst was raising his fees and although the husband's income had recently declined, he felt too embarrassed to discuss the financial problem with his analyst. The woman wanted to know if Mrs. Connell felt it would be permissible for her to call her husband's analyst and acquaint him with the facts. Mrs. Connell replied, "But you are in therapy. Why don't you discuss this with your analyst?" There was a moment of shocked silence, and then the woman said, "But, Mrs. Connell, this is a *reality* problem."

And indeed, this was the sort of situation I was in with my patients. I was ignoring the nightmare present they were in and focusing on the past. The immediate present was overwhelming and terrible. It was the fact aspect of their life. I was ignoring it, steering the therapy away from it, on the basis of a theory. This is not acceptable in science.

The second reason I became increasingly uncomfortable with the psychoanalytic approach was that I was making observations in my work that did not fit into the Freudian frame of reference.

In descriptions of patients and discussions of personality theory in the psychoanalytic literature, it has generally been very difficult to find statements of a positive nature. At that time if, in a psychoanalytically oriented staff conference, you used terms such as *courage, strength* (except *ego strength!*), *love, compassion, determination, religious awe,* you could depend on getting a hard time from your colleagues, almost always including references to counter-transference and suggestions that the speaker should consider going back and finishing his own analysis! (The problem I am describing took place over thirty years ago. The situation has somewhat changed at the present.)

Positive behavior was seen as resulting from combinations of ego defense mechanisms such as sublimation, reaction-formation, and overcompensation, all used to control pathological drives. Positive drives were seen as illusions. (The story is told of the secretary who got a job with an analyst, only to resign a few weeks later. When her friends asked why, she replied, "Because I couldn't win. If I came to work late, it was because I was hostile. If I came early, it was because I was anxious. If I arrived on time, it was because I was compulsive." The story may be apocryphal, but it is true that it would be foreign to the orientation of psychoanalytic theory to think that the secretary might have arrived early because she had extra work to do and took pride in doing a good job, on time because that is what she was paid for, or late because of an unforeseeable traffic jam.)

Gordon Allport has described this attitude as "a kind of contempt for the psychic surface of life. The individual's conscious report is rejected as untrustworthy and the contemporary thrust of his conduct is attributed to earlier formative stages." The educator Lawrence Brody refers to this as the "Oho Phenomenon." Whenever the patient says something, the therapist responds with an inward, "Oho, I know what *that* means." The individual has lost his right to be believed. (The widespread impact of the view that pathology is the natural and basic structure of the human personality is indicated by the modern, "sophisticated" mother who will feel at ease when her child is rambunctious. "That's sibling rivalry he's expressing. It's normal, and I know how to handle it." However, if the child is well-behaved, cheerful, cooperative, and happy, she becomes anxious and begins to wonder, "where is the hostility, and why can't he show it. What is he repressing?")

This was essentially the view of human nature that I brought to the psychotherapy with cancer patients. As I worked with them, however, I began to observe things that simply did not fit into this viewpoint. There is, when one is open oneself and works with people who are under terrible life threat, a curious nakedness. The usual defenses and masks tend to be dropped. One meets an "open" person. And, relating in this way to my patients, I found in them "courage" that was not a reaction-formation or a sublimation of anything else, "love" that was not Oedipal substitution, bone-deep "caring" and "altruism" and "compassion." I found myself *respecting* and *admiring* my patients, emotions that I had been in no way prepared for by my psychoanalytic training.

The basic faith of science is that if the facts do not fit the theory, it is the theory that must be abandoned. This is the underlying tenet of our science, although it is generally honored more in the breach than in the observance. Nevertheless, it was the cleft stick upon which I found myself. All my training and education to the contrary, I found my observations agreeing with Carl Rogers when he wrote:

> One of the most revolutionary concepts to grow out of our clinical experience is the growing recognition that the innermost core of man's nature, the deepest levels of his personality, the base of his "animal nature" is positive in character—is basically socialized, forward-moving, rational and realistic.[3]

A final reason I became increasingly uncomfortable with the psychoanalytic approach with patients with severe cancers is that at the end of a year and a half or so, I could see that the psychotherapy was having little if any effect on the development of the cancers. Although some patients seemed to feel better because of the therapy and all seemed to look forward to the sessions, they all died and, so far as I could tell, in about the same length of time as they would have died without the work we were doing.

The third area in which I had to transcend my training was the most basic aspect of psychotherapy. This is the problem of the underlying question that the therapist is asking. When I go to a therapist, he or she will almost invariably have a basic question: "What are the symptoms? What is hidden that is causing them? What can we do about it?'' Freud had first been a neurologist, and he took the basic question of clinical neurology ("What are the symptoms? Where is the hidden lesion that is causing them? What can we do about it?") and applied it to psychiatry. In both cases those large parts of either the nervous system or the personality that are functioning well or, at least, not causing symptoms are pretty much ignored.

Since Freud, all dynamic psychotherapy has rested on these questions. As I worked with my patients, however, I found that working on this path was not helpful in the sense that it did not affect the tumor growth. No matter how deeply we explored, no matter how well we proceeded in uncovering the hidden psychological lesions of the past, in finding what went wrong during early development and working the problem through, the cancers proceeded at the same pace. It was often very valuable psychologically for the patient to make these explorations; various *psychological* symptoms cleared up. But there seemed to be no relationship between what we were doing in the therapy sessions and the progression of the neoplasm.

Gradually, as I felt I was increasing my understanding of my patients, it became increasingly clear to me that mine was the wrong question for these people. It was too narrow, focused too much on pathology and the distortions of the past and childhood problems. I needed a question that would be *wider*, larger, and encompass more of their joys, hopes, and dreams for themselves. Over a period of time I began more and more to develop and to work with a different basic question in the psychotherapy. This was: "What is *right* about this person? What is the way for him to express his being, his creativity, his relating so that he uses the most of himself in the way most valid for him? What should her life be like so that she is glad to get up in the morning and glad to go to bed at night? So that when she is tired it is most often "good tired" and not (as one patient expressed it) the "yuck tired"? So that he uses the maximum of himself, from his feet to his scalp, in the way most right for him. What kind of being is *this* individual person—is she an elm, an oak, a willow, or an apple tree? What special kinds of soil will she best flourish in, what special combinations of sun and shade and so forth? What are the unique ways of being, relating, expressing, creating, valid for this person? What has blocked her perception of them in the past? What blocks her expression now? What is his "real name"; what has blocked his living under it? How can we move toward such full living of the self now?"

As patients understood the question I was asking of them and became involved in it, other changes began to occur. First, the *color* of their life seemed very often to change for the better. They became more concerned with life and living than with sickness and death. There was more zest and enthusiasm. Further, as they became committed to finding out the answers to these questions and to becoming *engagé* with the problem, they frequently began to respond better to whatever medical treatment they were on. Patients for whom there was only palliative treatment often showed a remarkable slowing of the tumor growth rate and, in some cases, a long-term reversal. Some of these patients with conditions for which at that time there was no treatment available at all (for example, one with an infiltrating brain tumor) are still alive and functioning well fifteen or twenty years later. By and large those who made these long-term remissions not only found out what their individual "song to sing" was, what their individual special "music to beat out" was like, but changed their lives to a greater or lesser degree to *sing* their own songs, to play their own music.

This method, which is described in other publications, and in which I have now been training psychotherapists for the past five years, does appear to be related to tumor growth. It appears to slow the rate of tumor development in the majority of patients who become *engagé*, who really begin working with it. Recently I followed up all those patients who had worked with me intensively during the four-year period starting eight years ago and going back to twelve years ago. I took from this group only those who were, by any reasonable medical standards, "terminal," that is, whom any experienced oncologist would have said at the time would almost certainly have been dead within a year at the outside. There are twenty-two patients who fit both these categories. Of them, twelve were still alive and functioning. It seems to me that this method achieves about 50 percent long-term remission with cancer patients who are not responding to presently known methods of mainline medicine.

Further, it appears to change the feeling tone of the great majority of the patients. Actively searching, as they are, for the meaning of their lives and for their own natural "style," they feel more like active explorers than like people who are very sick. The focus is on life, not illness or death. (Epictetus said, "Where life is, death is not," and the change in focus tends to have a very positive effect on the feelings.) Further, it is my strong *impression* (backed by no hard data) that it markedly tended to slow the rate of tumor development even in those who died.

That traditional psychotherapy led me to concentrate in the therapy on aspects of the situation that did not seem to be relevant; that I repeatedly observed things that did not fit into the system; and that it did not have a positive effect on tumor growth led me to reevaluate my view of what it means to be human and the psychoanalytic approach to personality.

From this distance, many years later, it seems to me that there is a strange distortion in our present view of Sigmund Freud and his contributions to our understanding and to our society. His name is a household word in the twentieth century. All serious modern psychotherapy rests its basic structure entirely on his contributions to knowledge. Major changes have been made in a dozen fields of learning, at least, because of his ideas. It is also true that Freud's genius has been consistently underestimated and that he has been given little or no credit for most of his fundamental contributions to science.

There are five basic concepts that Freud contributed to human understanding. Four of these appear to be permanent contributions to the conceptual tools we have with which to deal with reality. It is strange that he has generally been given credit only for the one that is likely to be soon outmoded—if it is not already. Or, at least, to be restricted to a small and special group of patients.

Here are what I consider to be Freud's greatest contributions:

1. The concept of a scientific method by means of which we can garden each other and help individuals past the stuntings, confusions, and bindings that so restrict our capabilities and our joys. The idea of such a method was unknown before him.
2. One example of this method—psychoanalytic psychotherapy. (This is the only contribution for which Freud is generally given credit.)
3. The concept that the way to study the mind successfully is not by the method developed by physics to study objects, but a very different, but valid, scientific method. Although this idea did not originate with Freud, he was the first to develop it to the point of real usefulness.
4. That the mind of a human being is:
   a. Dynamic, endlessly flowing, and moving;
   b. Complex and with various levels of consciousness and clarity constantly interacting; and
   c. Comprehensible.
5. That the same method can be used to comprehend the mind and behavior of human beings and to cure the individual's psychological problems.

It is not easy from the viewpoint of the present time to realize how revolutionary these ideas were when Freud brought them to our attention. They have become accepted and are part of the framework with which we view ourselves and others. But it took one of the greatest geniuses humankind has ever produced to find, develop, and clarify them and give us the basic tools and concepts with which to explore that tremendous and unknown frontier—the mind of human beings.

I have described in some detail the long research project on the psychosomatic aspects of cancer in order to clarify how

I had to change my own viewpoint in order to deal with the observations that I was making. It seems to me now, that in order to be able to understand the people I was seeing, people who were in great crisis, who were deeply in the human condition, I had to move to new concepts, to transcend my training in a number of ways. Further, it seems to me that the same necessity for change and growth is true for the field of psychology as a whole. Our subject *is* the human condition. If there is any justification for our existence, it is that we may further help understanding of the joys and fears, the terrors and exaltations, the quiet glows and the rocket flares of human existence. For this we need to grow far beyond the sterile laboratories where we spend much of our time. Not to forget what we have learned there, the rigor and beauty of the experimental methods, but to use these in the actual service of helping ourselves and others toward our potential.

It is not only in the laboratories where we must grow. It is also the narrow view of human beings that we use so often in the consultation room, the way we ignore the great aspects of life in our psychotherapies. With our overconcentration on pathology, with the tendency to "explain" *everything* on the basis of childhood distortions of reality and poor parental understanding, we have left large parts of what we are outside the door. If, for example, you ask the average psychotherapist why it is that with a human history in which people have repeatedly, and in large numbers, sacrificed psychological ease and physical comfort, and sometimes even survival itself, for spiritual ends; why it is that with this knowledge he or she pays no attention to spiritual factors in their therapy—you will probably get a confused look, some mutterings about this being all superstition and primitive activity we should wipe out as therapists. Further, you will probably get some suggestions about how you yourself obviously have not *worked through* your conflicts in this area and they will be glad to see you on a regular basis (perhaps at a professional discount for the fee) in order to help you work them through.

It is not only the spiritual aspects of human beings that

the modern therapist is rarely trained or equipped to deal with and to encourage and strengthen. It is also most of the other positive special aspects that make us more than animals and more than pathology. It is creativity and the love of the beautiful and of the true. It is "honor and faith and a sure intent." It is the search for the meaning of our existence. For a famous therapist to say, as one did, "Only philosophers and depressives ask 'What is the meaning of life?' " reduces the rest of us to a lower level than we are. Whether it is worse for the scientists who study human feelings and behavior to explain these as a bunch of connected reflex arcs, or to explain them as artifacts of an advanced computer, or to explain them as a collection of reaction-formations to pathological drives—which of these is worse for the effect it has on our attitudes toward ourselves and for the future of humankind—is a moot point indeed. All these things play a part in our being, but they no more explain them than the nuts and bolts that hold an automobile together explain and make up the automobile. Plato, long aeons ago, dealt with this problem in *The Phaedo*, and it will be necessary for psychologists to heed his words if they are ever going to succeed in their goal of helping us closer to our potential for splendor.

> *"There is surely a strange confusion of cause and conditions in all this," says Socrates. "It may be said, indeed, that without bones and muscles and all the other parts of the body I cannot execute my purposes. But to say that I do as I do because of them, and that this is the way in which the mind acts, and not from the choice of the best, is a very careless and idle mode of speaking. I wonder that they cannot distinguish the causes from the condition, which the many, feeling about in the dark, are always mistaking and misnaming." (Jowett translation)*

It is largely for this reason—that the scientists who should be responsibly working with the spiritual and aspirational aspects of human beings have rejected this area as unworthy of them— that those people who are seeking to find these parts of themselves go so frequently to the irresponsible, kooky, and predatory groups that pretend to have knowledge and working methods to help us grow in these ways. It is psychologists who are responsible for the immense growth and fat bank accounts of such groups as Dianetics, est, Mind Control, and the recent popularity of people who either hysterically believe, or else consciously pretend to be, "channelers" of discarnate spirits. (One of these—in California, of course—holds weekends of "channeling" for four hundred people at a time at four hundred dollars per person.) When psychologists realize that these positive aspects are real aspects of being human and that they are of tremendous importance to us, then people will not have to seek the solution to their needs at the hands of second-rate gurus, nuts, and those seeking to make personal fortunes out of these hopes and aspirations.

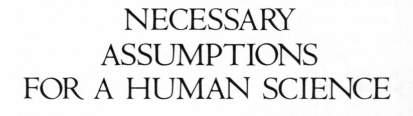

9

NECESSARY
ASSUMPTIONS
FOR A HUMAN SCIENCE

"If civilization is to survive, we must cultivate a science of human relationships, the ability of all people
. . . to live together . . . in the same world, at peace."
—1945 Jefferson Day speech of F.D.R. He did
not live long enough to deliver it.

Those who have believed most strongly in the method of the
physical sciences have long assumed that it was the only real
and legitimate source of knowledge. In the past hundred years,
our culture has generally assigned to the physical sciences the
mantle once humorously self-ascribed to the famous translator
of Plato who was Master of Balliol College at Oxford:

Yes, my name is Benjamin Jowett.
If a thing is known, I know it.
I am the Master of this College.
If I don't know it, it isn't Knowledge.

With this general assumption, any aspect of reality not amenable to investigation by this method was suspect and relegated to the outer darkness. Since this method is *only* applicable to measurable things, and to recurrent phenomena that could be predicted, the most important aspect of human beings—their consciousness and their individual meaningful behavior was believed to be outside of legitimate science and inquiry. Psychologists, being a part of their culture and believing in its conventional wisdom, therefore tried, and have been trying desperately, either to apply this method to human beings or to restrict psychological research to only those aspects of what it means to be human that *could* be so studied. Each failure has only made psychologists try harder. Their motto has seemed to be, "If the nut does not fit the bolt, then get a bigger wrench and force it harder."

> *And although in the hundred and twenty years or so, during which the ambition to imitate Science in its methods rather than in its spirit has now dominated social studies, it has contributed scarcely anything to our understanding of social phenomena, . . . demands for further attempts in this direction are still presented to us as the latest revolutionary innovations which, if adopted, will secure rapid, undreamed of progress.*[1]

A clarification and partial recapitulation of the central point of this book is in order here.

It is generally believed in our culture that there is *one* basic method of science. This is the method used in the physical sciences. With its stress on objectivity, predictability, analysis of the material into its basic components, quantification, and interpretation of the data in terms of how-a-machine-works, this method had led to tremendous progress.

What is not generally recognized today is that this methodological approach is valid only in certain realms of experience and is not valid in others. It is not valid for the exploration of human consciousness and human behavior, and its use in these realms has led to the present disaster of modern psychology.

For this realm of experience, human consciousness and human behavior, another method is necessary and was worked out at the end of the nineteenth and beginning of the twentieth century. This method and that worked out for the study of the natural sciences were described and contrasted in detail. A variety of names were applied to the two methods.

Ernest Rénan called them La Science de la Humanité and La Science de la Nature. The philosopher Wilhelm Dilthey called them Geisteswissenschaft and Naturwissenschaft. The philosopher Wilhelm Windelband and later the psychologist Gordon Allport called them Idiographic science and Nomothetic science.

These are two fundamentally different methodologies for scientific exploration. Both are equally valid for the realms of experience for which they have been designed and equally invalid if used in other realms. For example, La Science de la Nature is designed for the study of physical entities that can be perceived by the senses or by instrumental extensions of the senses. Used in this realm, it works very well indeed. It was not designed for the study of consciousness. Using it for this purpose because it worked so well in the realm for which it was designed is like driving a superb Rolls-Royce from San Francisco to New York City, and saying, upon arrival "The Rolls worked so well that I shall continue my journey by driving it to London." It is simply not designed for the next part of the trip and will quickly flounder as surely as did the field of psychology when it used the same reasoning and attempted the same maneuver with La Science de la Nature.

So far in this book I have shown how psychology went wrong in choosing the method of the physical sciences. This is not very difficult to do. One has only to point at the lack of results, the hundreds of ever-growing theories that have little if anything to do with each other, the irrelevance to human life of most of it, and the ever-increasing trivialization of the field. Far more important, however, is the need to go on from there;

to describe a more relevant and fruitful set of assumptions; a more useful method. It is this I propose to do from this point on.

Sooner or later each field of science must define and face its individual and unique critical task. For eighteenth- and nineteenth-century physics and chemistry, the task was "How does one deal with objective data?"—with the kind of observations that anyone could make and agree about what they were. A table is there to be seen and touched by anyone interested. We can agree on its length or on how to measure it. We can find ways we can accurately predict how much weight it can bear without breaking and how it will break if it does. We can, in short, all observe the same things and agree on what things we see, on how to define them, on how to measure them, and on what we mean by "explaining" them. The data all have *public* access.

Some of the explanations would involve constructs, things that could not be seen or touched. Molecules and atoms and electrons might have to be invented in order to explain the hardness and resilience of metals, but it was the hardness and resilience with which we were concerned, and these "observables" could be examined with our eyes and fingers (and with instruments to extend the sensitivity of these), on whose qualities and the amounts of these qualities we could agree. In Lewis Mumford's words:

> The method of the physical sciences [as developed in the seventeenth and eighteenth centuries] rested fundamentally upon a few simple principles. First: the elimination of qualities, and the reduction of the complex to the simple by paying attention only to those aspects of events which could be weighed, measured or counted; and to the particular kind of space-time regime that could be controlled and repeated—or, as in the case of astronomy, whose repetition would be predicted. Second: concentration upon the outer world, and the elimination or neutralization of the observer as respects the data with which he works. Third:

isolation; limitation of the field; specialization of interest and subdivision of labor.[2]

This method, ideal for the physical sciences, could not be adapted to the study of consciousness and behavior. Not only were none of the principles and restrictions that Mumford describes possible, but the very concept of *explanation*—what do we mean by "explaining" something?—had to be different. One statement of this is given by the historian R. G. Collingwood:

> *When a scientist asks, "Why did that piece of litmus paper turn pink?" he means, "On what kinds of occasions do pieces of litmus paper turn pink?" When a historian asks, "Why did Brutus stab Caesar?" he means, "What did Brutus think which made him decide to stab Caesar?" The cause of the event, for him, means the thought in the minds of the person by whose agency the event came about. . . .*[3]

The essential difference that makes the assumptions of the physical sciences irrelevant lies in the nature of the "critical task" of psychology. Until a science faces and defines its critical task and develops a method appropriate to it, it cannot make any real progress. The critical task of psychology has been to learn how to deal with data that are only in part open to public access—that is, data that include processes that cannot be observed by more than one person. The data of physics are all open to public access. The data of psychology are in part open to public access and the rest only open to *private access; they can only be observed by one person.* This does not make them any less *real* data; it only makes it necessary to find a method to study them.

My consciousness, my inner experience, by definition open only to one person, myself, to private access, is real. So is yours and if you doubt it, I suggest that you run, do not walk, to consult a good psychiatrist; it is indeed time to consider Thorazine or Haldol. But there is nothing in my consciousness that can be measured with a scale on which we both agree, that can be quantified in any way or that can be studied with the methods whose assumptions I defined so extensively earlier in this book.

To study consciousness and behavior, we need a different method with different assumptions. What might some of these assumptions be? Let us define them briefly and then look at them in somewhat greater detail. (I will then show some examples of how this method has been used fruitfully and well in the past and what it promises for the future.) What we are talking about here is a method for psychology adapted to the realm of experience, the kind of data we are actually dealing with. When a discipline does this, formalizes and adapts its relevant method, it really becomes a science and begins to move forward.

The basic assumptions for the study of human consciousness and individual behavior are as follows:

1. All divisions within the data of the field, divisions such as conscious-unconscious, cultural and family influence, nature-nurture, and structure and function, are artificial and for descriptive purposes only. They are *heuristic*; that is, they are not "real", but we impose them on the data in order to make it easier for us to study and conceptualize the data and to communicate our ideas. There are no separate and discrete parts within or between the person's consciousness and behavior. My thoughts do not end and then my feelings start. Nor is there a stopping place between your memories and your present perceptions and evaluations of what you perceive.

2. Any experiment in psychology must include, as one of the major variables, the total psychological and social situation of the subject, and include the relationship with the experimenter. This must be stated in each report, as there is no "standard" relationship or psychological situation. There may be standard conditions of air pressure and gravity for a

chemical experiment, and as a consequence it may be unnecessary to "state" them; there are no such standard
conditions for a psychological experiment.

The experimental psychologist can never be a "trans-
parent witness" (as the medieval manuscript advises us to
be), because he is dealing with an *interpersonal situation* in
any experiment he does. Even if all the instructions to the
subject are given by a computer, still the computer is *his*
representative and *he* is the one who provides its status and
authority. No laboratory situation is an individual one; each
has a subject and an experimenter and the attitude of the
subject toward the experimenter influences his laboratory
behavior.

3. The study of psychology is the study of the individual's consciousness and the individual's meaningful behavior. These
are two realms of experience. The realm of meaningless (reflex) behavior is a third realm of experience, and the study
of groups of individuals a fourth. As above, these are only
heuristic divisions; the organism acts as a whole (including
its reflexes and group behavior).

4. All behavior has a purpose, and this must be a factor in
describing it. "Purposeless" behavior and "uncaused"
chemical reactions mean the same thing—that we do not
know at least one of the major variables involved in what
is going on. Behavior is an attempt to accomplish something.

The "cause" of an action, the "explanation," is made
up of two elements. First, the situation or state of things
existing. This is what is going on in the immediate neighborhood *as it is perceived* by whoever is doing the action.
(How humans react to things is much more due to the human than to the thing. An ordinary hammer and a jack-
hammer, an aneroid and a mercury barometer have nothing
much in common except for the *purpose* for which humans
think they can be used.) The second is the purpose or the
state of things wished to be obtained. Both of these elements must be considered in any explanation in psychology.

They depend on each other, and neither has any meaning in terms of the action without the other.

5. Any single-system explanation of a process of consciousness or of individual, meaningful behavior is a serious distortion of the human condition. "Explanation" must be in terms of combining ways of description rather than opting for one of them. Anna Karenina did not throw herself under the train because she was rejected by her lover. This was one factor, perhaps a triggering factor, in her suicide, but her culture of origin, her family subculture, her personality structure, her total life experience, and her genetic inheritance also are a part of the pattern that resulted in her death. We understand more deeply by understanding more widely. Think of a Navaho, a flower-child, a yuppie, a psychopath, or a Norwegian in situations structurally similar to that of Anna K. Each would have behaved differently. When we read Tolstoy's novel, the reason we comprehend Anna K's final action is that the author has already taught us about a wide variety of the influences that helped shape her and it. Understanding a particular sequence of consciousness or behavior is an endless process that consists of relating the particular sequence under study to larger and larger sequences involving more and more of the organism, its history, and the social environment to which it is responding. There are only convenient stopping places in this process, not realistic ones. We stop the process of explanation either at a convenient place we have determined in advance or at the point where our curiosity flags. These are artificial points only, and this must be kept in mind.

6. As long as a process or event is open to private access only, that is, as long as we are studying consciousness, it is not quantifiable in principle. Quantification necessarily involves agreement on the exact meaning and definition of basic measurement units, and this is simply not possible in private-access realms of experience.

Defining units of aspects of consciousness may be fun, but it is simply not useful. To ask "How many 'Romeos' do

I have in my love for her?" is an interesting but pointless exercise.

7. The realms of experience studied by psychology, individual behavior and consciousness, do not permit exact prediction. This is, in part, because the same precise situation cannot be repeated and so the type of laws that make this type of prediction possible cannot be developed. Where an individual shows repetitious and stereotyped behavior of the sort that makes precise prediction possible (in even a very limited area), we can be certain that we are dealing with a severely damaged individual. Further, no individual is precisely like, is identical to, any other. Similarly, no individual remains the same over a period of time. Our inner experience differs from that of all others and is constantly changing.

8. The actions of an individual depend in large part on his *history*. This is much less true in the physical sciences, where one lump of lead behaves pretty much like another, has pretty much the same properties, irrespective of whether it has been in sunlight or in darkness, or whether it has been isolated or in the company of other lumps of lead, for the past ten years. This is not true of a person. Both history and properties play a part in the reaction of both, but the emphasis is very markedly different.

Generally speaking, we do not require understanding of the history of a physical system to understand its actions. It tends to make little real difference if our car came to us from Detroit on a train or on a truck. We do need to understand the history of an individual to comprehend his present activity and to make general predictions for the future.

9. The goals of a science of psychology are very different from the goals of physics and chemistry. The goals of the physical sciences are a conception of the cosmos that permits ever-greater mathematical prediction and ever-greater control of the entities and processes studied. The goal of psychology is the kind of understanding that will help individuals to live

fuller, richer, and more exuberant lives. As the methods of a science must, for the sake of progress, be adapted to the type of material studied, so the experiments and research of a science must be adapted to its goals. If a study does not use appropriate methods or is not oriented toward appropriate goals, it is, at best, a waste of time.

10. Human beings are a symbol-using class of life and define their goals (as well as a large part of their immediate perceptions of what is going on around them) by, and in, symbols. Generalizing to a symbol-using class of life from a non-symbol-using class is a tour de force of extremely doubtful validity. Similarities are much more apparent than real. Thus, human beings cannot be understood in any meaningful or fruitful way through the study of animals.

Generalizing from machine behavior to that of humans is an even more fruitless activity and can have little more effect than amusing the psychologist who is doing the generalizing. Conceivably (although I doubt it), a computer could be designed that would write acceptable poetry. But there is not the possibility of a computer that, after encoding and recording a poem, would actively desire to buy a bunch of flowers for another computer and to live with it forever. Or a computer that could experience awe in a cathedral or that, falling apart of old age, would wish deeply for the comforting presence of its mother.

These are the basic assumptions for a science of psychology—for the scientific study of human consciousness and behavior. However, before we go on with the analysis of these two approaches, the question arises—"Would shifting to Idiographic science, as the method for psychology really make any difference? Isn't all this theory pretty far removed from human life?" Let us come to grips with this question by giving one example of how psychology would be different.

For the example we take the final written examination for the Ph.D. The student has completed his coursework and internship; as part of his preparation he has done a good deal of self-exploration and has demonstrated his expertise in one other approach to the human condition from that found in the textbooks of psychology. He has passed the first days of the examination in which he has been tested in his knowledge of the problems of ethics in the field of psychology, the history of psychology and its relationships with other fields, of the developmental stages and tasks that an individual in his own culture faces, and so forth. Now comes the final part of his examination. He is given one question and two entire days to answer it. The question has six parts. He is given the first two parts on the first day and the other four on the second. This is the test.

1. Choose a person whom you know very well, either personally, from biography, or from fiction. Describe him or her from the viewpoint of B. F. Skinner, Jean-Paul Sartre, Sigmund Freud, Alfred Adler, Feodor Dosteovsky, Henry James, D. O. Hebb, Carl Jung, Carl Rogers, Kurt Lewin, William Stern, Karen Horney, Arthur Miller, Salvador Minuchin, Erik Erikson, Kurt Goldstein, Andreas Angyal, Henry Murray, Victor Frankl, Jane Austen, V. I. Lenin, Robert Havighurst, Aaron Beck, Neal Miller, Otto Rank. (Choose 4.)

2. Combine these into a description of the person that will be most useful to a potential employer, to a troubled spouse, to a psychiatrist, to a court judge, to a vocational counselor, for a three-paragraph entry in an encyclopedia. (Choose 2.)

3. Describe the tests and techniques you might use to increase your understanding of this person. Tell why you chose each one.

4. Design or report on a laboratory experiment that would help you learn more about this person. You can either design a new study or use one from the professional literature. Justify your choice.

5. From a psychological viewpoint, in what ways is your subject most like all members of the human species? In what ways is he or she most like other members of his subculture? In what ways is he unique, most like himself?

6. What in you, in your own experience and personality struc-

ture, made you choose this particular person to write about in such detail? How do you think this influenced your conclusions? How do you feel about this?

This is the type of final examination a student trained in an Idiographic psychology would be likely to be given. Given the choice of a psychologist trained to pass an examination like this, and one trained in the usual university program in psychology, which would you prefer to hire as a personnel specialist, as a school psychologist for the school your child is in, as a psychotherapist, as your teacher of psychology, or as a consultant on a social action program?

THE TWO METHODS
OF SCIENCE

It need scarcely be emphasized that nothing we shall have to say is aimed against the methods of Science in their proper sphere or is intended to throw the slightest doubt on their value. But to preclude any misunderstanding on this point, we shall, whenever we are concerned not with the general spirit of disinterested inquiry but a slavish imitation of *Science*, speak of "scientism" or the "scientististic prejudice." ... these terms ... describe, of course, an attitude which is decidedly unscientific ... since it involves a mechanistic and uncritical application of habits and thoughts to fields different from those in which they were conceived.[1]

The two methods, La Science de la Humanité and La Science de la Nature, have much in common. They might be compared to the long and serious explorations of the human condition of the ancient Greeks and of the ancient Hebrews—so to speak of the families of Zeus and of Jehovah. These two share an alphabet clearly arising from one spring—the first starts with alpha, beta, and the second starts with aleph, beth, for example. The two great explorations satisfy many of the same needs. Their differences are profound, however, and neither is derivative of the other. The great Greek play *Oedipus Rex* and the magnificent Hebrew Psalms of David the King each stands on its own feet as an attempt to understand and describe what it means to be a human being. Although both may stand on the shoulders of a common ancestor, neither stands on the shoulders of the other or depends on it for validity.

An art form, such as painting, is not a failed science. Neither is science a failed art form. Both satisfy human needs. Both are part of our quest to survive, as individuals and as a species, and to become more at home with ourselves with others, and with that general nature of which we are a part.

The significant differences between the two types of science have not been clearly understood very often in recent years. I will show one way of organizing them here in order that they may be more easily compared and contrasted and so that in our work in psychology we can see clearly which method we wish to use in any given circumstance. This is extremely important to us if we wish to make actual progress.

Each method is ideal for certain purposes and useless for others. Nomothetic science is completely, ideally, and only adapted to the Space-Time-Energy-Matter universe (the STEM realm of experience). Taking it to other realms of experience is similar to equipping and training your troops for desert warfare and then sending them off to fight in the Antarctic.

At this point, we might consider three major kinds of differences between these two scientific methods. These are:

1. The permanence of facts.
2. The goals of science.
3. The realm of inquiry in science.

In the rest of this chapter, I will discuss these in more detail.

I. THE PERMANENCE OF FACTS

In La Science de la Nature, facts are truths for a time only. Their truth is transitory. Much of what was "truth" for eighteenth- and nineteenth-century science is now superstition. Many facts are outmoded or else their province is now severely restricted. We no longer believe in the existence of *caloric fluid*, in *bleeding* in medicine (except for a few, very rare conditions), or in the existence of the luminiferous *ether*. These, and a host of others, were proven scientific facts in the past and are no longer regarded as valid. (The efficacy of Guiacum in the treatment of syphilis is another example. Long considered a well-proven and extensively documented treatment method, no physician would dream of using it today. It is "known" to be medically useless.)

Another major class of facts in the science that deals with "objective" truths is that comprised of those facts that are still regarded as "true," but whose province is very much reduced. We still believe that Newton's equations and "facts" are valid, but they are no longer seen as covering the wide and universal ground that Newton and scientists of the next two and a half centuries thought that they did. Instead of being "facts" for the entire cosmos, we now see them as true only for that narrow region in which our senses operate. When we get into the very large and fast, the range where relativity "facts" and equations are true, they no longer are valid. And when we get into the range of events too small for the senses to operate, even theoretically, the quantum realm of experience, they are also inapplicable.

Even the revered Second Law of Thermodynamics, which physicists once thought to be valid throughout all of reality, no longer is believed to have this universal reign. Once we regarded it as inexorably leading the total cosmos to its "heat death," the sterile, formless, final form of the universe in which each particle of matter would be at equal distances from those nearest to it and so remain, inert, immovable, forever. This grisly prediction, once believed to be inevitably true, is no longer generally accepted in science. The Second Law is now seen as inexorable only within that narrow range within which the senses of humankind can operate. Beyond the extremes of the too-small-to-perceive-even-theoretically and the too-large-or-too-fast-to-perceive-even-theoretically, this law does not operate. Neither does it exist in the realm of consciousness.

The mechanical model and the laws of mechanics were once believed to cover all of existence. Today we see that they also are restricted to those areas that we can, actually or theoretically, observe with our senses.

Thus "facts" in the La Science de la Nature are transitory and subject to becoming either outmoded or severely limited in their range of coverage and applicability.

In La Science de la Humanité, on the other hand, facts do not become obsolete. Our understanding of the rage of Clytemnestra at the murder of her daughter and her subsequent killing of Agamemnon is no less valid today than it was when Aeschylus wrote his great play. Our insights may have deepened and we may understand that she would have felt and behaved differently if she had been raised in another culture (a concept that would have been quite foreign to a Greek of the classical period), but we still feel empathetic with her and comprehend her feeling and behavior.

Shakespeare's *Richard the Third* is as valid today as it was in the sixteenth century. We can, today, see Richard with more conceptual tools at hand than the Elizabethans who crowded the Globe Theatre in Shakespeare's day, but we do not feel and know his desire for kingship any more than they did. We and they respond similarly to the ruthless ambition and need for positive response of one who has been crippled from birth in a world where physical prowess and handsomeness are two of the most respected assets; who feels he has been cheated of his birthright in other ways as well; and who believes that he has a right to any action necessary to restore the balance, even if these actions are against his own moral beliefs and those accepted as "right" by his time. We see more in the play now, we can bring the wisdom and understanding of a Freud and an

Adler to bear on Richard's motivation, but we do not feel deeper empathy or *respond* with greater intensity. The play is as valid as ever. Its *facts* have not been superseded by new facts nor has their province become more limited. We simply see more deeply and more widely.

The writing of Plato on the human capacity to act for good or evil is still valid although we know far more about human motivation than he did. The writing of Democritus on atomic structure is not.

A Capra photograph of the horrors of war is still as valid as ever even though it is in black and white and modern color photography adds new dimensions to our perception and response. Similarly Goya's paintings and etchings tell us a great deal about the suffering and human desolation war causes. With new insights into painting and new techniques, Picasso's *Guernica* tells us additional things. The interviews and research of the psychiatrist Robert Jay Lifton further deepen our understanding. Dostoevsky's insights into the nature of man and his capacity for good and evil are as valid in the twentieth as they were in the nineteenth century and will be equally valid in the twenty-first (a prediction we can make about very few facts in physics and chemistry). Achilles sulking in his tent tells us as much that is true of the nature of love and loss as it did in the fifth century B.C. In La Science de la Humanité, new "facts" are added and insights deepened. Our knowledge of human consciousness and behavior has been added to by the concept, and studies of, cognitive dissonance; by studies such on regression under stress; by research on peak experiences, by Erik Erikson's work on the life cycle; by Arthur Miller's *Death of a Salesman* and by Freud's *Mourning and Melancholia*. These help us to move ever closer to the "Disciplined Subjectivity" that anthropologist Gregory Bateson told us is so crucial for psychology. We have added much to the concepts of the previous centuries, but they have not lost their validity. We have, instead, deepened them.

II. THE GOALS OF SCIENCE

In La Science de la Nature, our goals are forever and ever wider and more systematically ordered systems of facts and their relationships. We want here to know more and more facts and to relate them to each other in ever-expanding structures until, theoretically at any rate, we find the grand equation that connects the whole cosmos in one coherent, beautiful pattern. It was for this general theory that Einstein spent the last years of his life searching. Further, we seek, by means of this understanding, to *control* the world of things. We believe that as we come to greater understanding, we come to greater and greater control. There is, theoretically, no limit to the control we envisage, as there is no limit to the understanding we seek. When the science-fiction writer describes the men and women of the future being able to control the course of development of the stars and the placement of the planets, this is entirely consistent with our present thought.

The goal of Idiographic science, on the other hand, is to enrich human life and to make it more full, varied, restful.

In La Science de la Humanité, we search for deeper and deeper understanding, for the ability to feel more and more empathy with individuals. We are not so concerned with facts and their relationships, since the more deeply we understand, the fewer facts there are. Consciousness is indeed a seamless garment with no discrete elements. We are concerned rather with our own consciousness being able to "feel the feelings and think the thoughts" of another person, to so expand our own inner life that it is true that "nothing human is alien to me." In this way, with this type of understanding, we can more accurately comprehend what another person is likely to feel, think, and do in the future and in other circumstances. We can also perceive how to help free another person from his or her inner blockages and neurotic bindings by comprehending what he or she needs to be free. This is, after all is said and done, how a good psychotherapist works. He uses whatever techniques his school or cult has taught him to work toward those moments of such empathic understanding that he truly sees the world through his patients' eyes, feels their pain and the inner walls and neurotic bindings that limit them, and, with the therapist's own trained and expanded consciousness, knows what is needed or what must be done to help them grow toward their own health and optimum functioning.

Thus there are two meanings to the term *understanding,* each applicable to one form of science. In the science of things, the term means more and more clear analytic knowledge of the parts and ways that they are related. In the science of human beings, the term means an ever-deepening empathy, a "standing under" the same sky and on the same earth as the other person so that we may live in his world with him and comprehend his motivations and responses. The old American Indian saying, "Never judge any other person until you have walked a mile in his moccasins," is relevant here.

We do not know the laws of human behavior, but we can understand them. Chamberlain changed his behavior toward Hitler after Hitler broke his word and marched into Czechoslovakia. We do not understand the laws that governed this change of Chamberlain's and do not believe that there are such laws, yet we understand quite well what happened. I understand someone else through a reliving of their experience, not by means of analyzing their behavior into laws. I comprehend Don Quixote very well, but we have no laws, nor will we ever have them, that define his behavior. In Dilthey's words "We always understand far more than we know."

Both Idiographic and Nomothetic science are, in principle, asymptotic—we can never reach the end of our search in either. There is always more to learn, whether we are training to be empathic with another human being or to understand the laws of hydrodynamics. This is easy to see in physical science: a scientist may spend his life in a narrow field of research and find that as knowledge grows in his area of specialization, he can barely, or not at all, keep up with the old and new journals directly affecting his work. All experienced research specialists have had that experience.

In Idiographic science this may be harder to understand: we all have had the experience after an emotional contact with another person (or character in a book, play, or film) of believing that *we really understood* that person. And yet, there is always more. I recall a repeated incident during World War II. We were working with soldiers who had had such traumatic battle experiences that they had broken down in their ability to function. We called this "combat fatigue"; there were a large number of cases in the hospitals.

One technique we used then was interviews during which the patient was under sodium pentothal. With this and some hypnotic techniques, we were able to have the soldier reexperience the traumatic battle experiences—to live through them again. Combined with support, reassurance, and suggestion, this approach was often very helpful as a treatment method.

Repeatedly the following events would occur (this was in the United States, far from the actual scenes of combat): The soldier would be lying on a bed. Standing next to the bed would be a nurse, and a psychologist or a psychiatrist. As the soldier reexperienced the battle scene, it was often so "real" that we observers found ourselves bending down, "ducking" to avoid mortar shells that had actually fallen months before and thousands of miles away. Our empathic relation with the soldier was so strong that our involuntary reflexes tried to save us from the explosions and shrapnel he was emotionally experiencing and remembering. It is hard to imagine a stronger empathy and comprehension.

But none of us developed combat fatigue. We knew we experienced only *part* of what the soldier had. In spite of being from the same culture and the same wartime period of history, in spite of our training and our desire to *be with* the soldier, in spite of the tremendous realism of the pentothal-opened and -driven experience, we could go only so far. The best of us could go the furthest, and so made the best and most successful psychotherapists. Our deeper comprehension made it possible for us to communicate in more helpful ways with the soldier and to understand more what this particular person needed to come to his version of fullest and most zestful functioning. But none of us reached, or even glimpsed, a limit. There was always the possibility of comprehending more fully, of empathizing more completely.

In this chapter, I am discussing three aspects of the differences between the two kinds of science—La Science de la Humanité and La Science de la Nature. A more concrete illustration of these differences may be illustrated by what is certainly the most well-known case in the history of psychotherapy—Freud's case of "Dora."[2]

Dora was the younger of two children; her brother was a year and a half older. Their father was in his late forties and had suffered from a number of illnesses throughout his life. Freud had treated him for the consequences of a syphilitic infection; his symptoms had cleared up entirely. Four years later he brought his daughter to Freud, and psychotherapy had been recommended. At that time, she rejected the notion. Two years later, however, she returned and stayed in treatment with Freud for three months.

When treatment began, Dora was eighteen years old. She had been suffering from a variety of hysterical symptoms since the age of eight. Freud says that she suffered from the commonest of all somatic and mental symptoms—breathing difficulties, nervous cough, loss of voice (sometimes for five weeks at a time), possible migraine, depression, hysterical unsociability, suicidal ideas, and a general dissatisfaction with life.

Dora's mother was described by Freud as a woman suffering from what he called "housewife psychosis"—that is, a woman who was so wrapped up in the details of housekeeping chores that she was unable to relate to any of her family.

Dora's parents had become friendly with another family, the K's. As soon became clear in the course of Dora's analysis, Dora's father had begun an affair with Mrs. K, as compensation for the coldness of his wife. Mr. K had made sexual advances to Dora and had wanted to marry her. Dora's illness was connected with her love for her father, the proposals of Mr. K, and her homosexual love for Mrs. K, as well. All this, in turn, was tied up with her own family situation—that is, her Oedipal conflict. It is to be noted, however, that at this time (1901) Freud did not trace the conflict back to the childhood Oedipal period, between three and five, but contented himself with working out the difficulties that had arisen in the period of Dora's adolescence.

As already noted, Dora remained in treatment for three months, at the end of which time she abruptly broke off without explanation. Fifteen months later, however, she returned for a consultation. It appeared that she had made some symptomatic improvement, although hysterical symptoms of one kind or another continued to crop up.

Freud's *method* in this case was the method of La Science de la Humanité. He started out by asking "Who is *this* person?" Then he asked, "What can we say about persons who show neurological symptoms without neurological changes, that is, hysterics?" Finally, "How does this hysteric differ from other hysterics?"

It was in this paper that Freud first illustrated in detail one of his tremendous contributions—the idea that neurosis is psychological in nature and must be comprehended in psychological terms. This contribution made further advances in our understanding of neurosis possible. (Today we know that we can often block the *symptoms* of a neurosis by means of chemical medications, but to understand, and ultimately cure a neurosis, we must remain in the psychological area.)

The realm of inquiry in this study was the individual person. Freud was concerned with how Dora perceived and defined her life situation and what her goals were. He pointed out in detail that each person is capable of defining the situation differently and of having different goals on various "levels" of personality; feelings and behavior are not simply determined by the consciously held definitions and goals. (This idea was a tremendously revolutionary one in 1901.) Dora's unconscious attraction to Herr K, and her unconscious desire to have a sexual relationship with him was a major factor in influencing her toward the production of hysterical symptoms. In this realm of inquiry, Freud demonstrated, conscious and unconscious purposes and goals are as absolutely necessary to take into account as are mass and inertia in the realm of inquiry studied by mechanical engineering.

In the realm of inquiry of the individual human being—his feelings, perceptions, and actions—there are no exact laws, but we can make useful generalizations to a class of persons. As we learn more and more about a specific type of paintings—say, Impressionist paintings—we can say more and more and make more and more predictions about paintings in this genre, even as we are completely aware that each painting is unique and its composition could not—in principle—be predicted in advance even if we know what the subject is and who is the painter. Before they were painted, it would be impossible to say what a specific Monet "Waterlilies" or a Derain "London Bridge" would be like, but if we know enough about art history in general, and about Impressionism in particular, we can understand much about this class of paintings and about both how these two specific works of art are like others of this class and how they are different. The essential test of any science or art is its power to aid in transformations. Today our power to do this in this particular realm of inquiry is greater because of this study and the work of which it was a part.

In psychology, no specific laws have been found. (Even the one that Freud once thought he had discovered—all hysteria has a sexual basis—has long been abandoned.) We have, however, come to a deeper understanding of not only human beings in general, but of hysterics in particular. We can now feel empathy more deeply with them, generally predict the future course of an individual and help him more. In this study a previously unknown syndrome is explored in depth. No rules are found, no laws are defined, but we know far more than we did before it was done.

Another aspect of La Science de la Humanité illustrated by "Dora" is the permanence of facts. Freud's insights of 1901 are still valid today, but with new tools and concepts, we com-

prehend far more about her today than he could. We are enriched, deepened in our understanding, far beyond what was
possible for him.

As we read Freud's 1905 publication of the case, we know
we are in the presence of genius. We stare in amazement as he
probes deeply into Dora's misery and her life with his magnificent intelligence and sees and follows clues that we would have
passed by unnoticing. Freud is concerned chiefly with the level
of personality we would call today the "ego defenses"—how she
represses and distorts feelings in an attempt to ease her pain.
He brings a new comprehension to her behavior and to many
human myths and legends. We understand far more after the
case was published than we did before.

But—there is so much more we know today than he did.
We can see Dora in a far richer context. We understand family
dynamics, genetic pressures, social class patterns, cultural influences, developmental tasks and opportunities, in ways no one
could have in 1901. If twenty years afterward Freud could say
that he considered his original theory about Dora "correct but
incomplete" and that he had missed much of the transference
and its importance, what would he have said eighty years later?
Indeed, if he were alive today, Freud, with his emphasis on the
growth and constant development of our human understanding,
would clearly be labeled an "anti-Freudian."

In terms of the family influences on Dora, today we see
these as a web of pressures and opportunities operating in a
"field." As psychiatrist Philip Rieff notes, we see Dora as

> the sick daughter has [a sick mother and] a sick father who
> has a sick mistress, who has a sick husband who proposes
> himself to the sick daughter as her lover. Dora does not
> want to hold hands in this charmless circle.[3]

Freud saw some of the influence of the parents on Dora, but
not the family Gestalt, not in the field-dynamics terms we would
use today. In his time the prevailing (and essentially only) scientific concept was of individual action and reaction. Despite

the work of Mach and a few others, the concept of the field was little known.

Today we would see Dora, not only as an inseparable part of the total family but also as "the bellringer," the one who, by moving into a visible pathology, signals to the world that the entire Gestalt is badly distorted and that help is needed. These concepts were unknown in 1901.

Today we would also ask many other questions about her. What, for example, was her genetic reactivity level? Since the work of René Spitz and of Margaret Friess, we know that the general reactivity level of a person is genetically determined. Friess has described what happens if you take a one-day-old child and place it on a scale to weigh it and one toe touches the cold metal. One child will scream, turn red, arch its back, and very strongly react with all the resources at its command. Another child will not react to the touch and, even if you at that moment accidentally knock over an instrument stand and the room is full of noise and excitement, will simply lie there contentedly. Friess calls these two types "wave-makers" and "wave-riders." The first, she says, will cause tidal waves and hurricanes if you place it in a quiet woodland pool on a calm day. The second will bob comfortably and peacefully on the waves of an ocean storm. These inborn differences, we know today, play a role in how a person reacts to whatever situation in which he finds himself for the rest of his life. What was Dora's general level of response? What part did it play in the development of her personality and pathology?

Today we would also ask what Dora's most natural ways of being, relating, creating were, so that when she expressed herself in these ways, it was with her maximum "song to sing," her "music to beat out"? What were these patterns of personality expression and what had blocked them? Could they be found and released? This additional conceptual tool gives the modern psychotherapist much greater power to comprehend and help than was available at the beginning of the century. At that time the definition of the goal of psychotherapy, as expressed by Freud, was "To remove the unique pains of the pa-

tient and return him to that unhappiness common to mankind."
Today we have an additional goal, which, as formulated by
Karen Horney, is "To help the patient take his uniqueness, his
individuality, his neurosis, from in front of the eyes where it
acts as blinders and move it around to the back of the neck
where it acts as an outboard motor."

We would also ask today about the social class and the
culture and subculture that Dora was raised in. How, for example, did it define female sexuality? What were the developmental tasks assigned to each age group? Dora was fourteen
years old when Herr K made his first sexual advances to her,
advances that she found so unconsciously attractive and consciously repellent that she refused to spend any further time
alone with him; but she was also generally ill when he was
absent from the family grouping and recovered when he returned. (This was in contrast to her mother, who was generally
ill when the father was at home and well when he was away
on trips.) What did the cultural and social class norms Dora
knew say about a woman's sexual feelings at fourteen—the age
of Juliet in a very different culture? What was acceptable and
what was not?

Because we would see Dora in a much wider context than
Freud could, we can *comprehend* her much more deeply. Freud's
"facts" have not become "untrue," nor have they become limited in scope as have the Newtonian time and space definitions.
Instead they are *enriched* and *deepened* by knowledge of more
concepts and approaches to hysteria. It is an endless process.
Future generations will comprehend Dora more deeply than we
do, but the facts that Freud uncovered will still be true.

III. THE REALM OF INQUIRY IN SCIENCE

In Idiographic science, the science of human beings, we
can only deal with the feelings and behavior of individuals. It
is only with the individual that we can even hope to feel empathy. I can be empathic, if only in theory, with a specific

Frenchman. I cannot be empathic with a crowd of Frenchmen, or with "France" or "Europe." (I can never even hope to be empathic with a machine.) I can describe the behavior of a mob: I can be empathic with specific individuals who are in it. La Science de la Humanité is the science of the behavior and consciousness of individuals. In Nomothetic science, La Science de la Nature, I do not seek to be empathic, I seek to describe, to understand the parts of the entity I am studying and the relationship of these parts. I seek, by means of this, to be able to control the present and future actions of this entity and others of the same class.

I can do this with a machine, with a mob, with "the French," with "Europe," at least theoretically. It is clear that the individual and the group of individuals are in different realms of experience and demand different methods of study. Science means something different when we are studying the individual and when we are studying groups of individuals.

This is the reason that the study of how to predict and control the behavior of groups has (as seen in advertising) progressed so much more rapidly than the attempts of psychology to predict and control the behavior of individuals. The method used in both cases was the method of Nomothetic science, and this method was applicable only to the study of groups, not to the study of individuals. Further, the *goals* of advertising— prediction and control—are applicable only to the science that deals with groups, not the science that deals with individuals.

There is a basic difference between the "inside" and the "outside" of an event. The outside is concerned with physical action and movement. It asks "How?" The inside is concerned with thought and feeling. It asks "Why?" Caesar died on the Senate portico floor. That is the *outside*. The *inside* concerns that deep difference of feeling about the Roman Republic between Caesar and the assassins. He believed it to be an evil; they believed it to be a good. He wanted to destroy it; they wanted to protect it. He hated it; they loved it.[4]

Nomothetic science is concerned with the outside of events; Idiographic science with both the inside *and* the outside. This is why the term *purpose* is anathema and meaningless in physics and chemistry and is essential in psychology.

To understand behavior, we must regard it from two viewpoints at the same time: The *causa ut*, its purpose, the state of things wished to be brought about, and the *causa quod*, the perceived state of things, what the individual believes is going on in the immediate neighborhood.

There is no contradiction between these two types of explanation. Both are of equal validity, and neither rules out the other. Konrad Lorenz writes of the ". . . basically erroneous belief that a process which is causally determined cannot, at the same time, be goal directed." He points out that if my car breaks down in the middle of an important journey, I am made very aware that there is a purpose to my trip and there is a causal process that makes my car go.[5]

One can thus distinguish two radically different types of explanation. The first relates the event to its antecedent conditions. The second to the reasons for performing the action. The first applies to metal fatigue causing the collapse of a bridge. The second to Columbus crossing the ocean. The second type of explanation—finding a shorter route to the Indies—does not involve any laws or lawlike generalizations, but places the action in a unique context in which the action seems a rational approach to the problem.

A response is not to the antecedent conditions—what was going on in the immediate neighborhood just before the action—but to the situation *as defined by the person doing the action.* We do not say the problem was correctly evaluated, the person may have been wrong or crazy, but that he based his action on his evaluation. Columbus was wrong—the eastern route was shorter and better to the Far East. In fact, his conviction does appear rather like an obsession. Napoleon had a reason for the disposition of his heavy dragoons at Waterloo. The reason was based on a faulty map he believed to be valid. It did not show the sunken road that destroyed much of his cavalry.

However, the reason for ordering the charge of the dragoons was that it seemed to him the best way to accomplish his goal. The antecedent conditions—the "causal" explanation—gives an entirely different set of answers than does the "rational" explanation. With a causal explanation we might explain Columbus's crossing as due to an overcompensation for an inferiority complex because of his mother's preference for his older brother, or to an inborn human need for self-realization. The social sciences, and psychology in particular, must have both sorts of explanation. It must be kept clear that these are two different scientific methods and are of equal value. Each applies to certain kinds of problems and certain kinds of data. The general trend of psychology has been for psychologists to ascribe the behavior of others to "causal" factors and use causal explanations for them, and ascribe their own behavior to rational (purposeful) factors and to use rational explanations for what we do. If the science of psychology is to make any progress, this strange and illegitimate dichotomy between the psychologist and the "others" has to be abandoned. We can only comprehend the consciousness and behavior of other persons to the degree we accept our own humanity.

Unfortunately, as the social philosopher Theodore Roszak has written, ". . . Behaviorism the most scientized form of psychology and the school that dominates our universities, does not even give us a starting point for self-examination. It displaces experience with experiment."[6]

SUMMARY
AND CONCLUSIONS

This book started with the question of why psychology has not been seen as a useful tool to solve the desperate problems of our time. That a scientific culture—one that habitually turns to science to solve important problems—should not turn to the science of human thought and behavior when its main and existence-threatening problems are in this area is indeed startling.

The conclusion reached here was that psychology has so thoroughly sold its birthright, has so completely abandoned any real contact with human existence, that it is widely believed in our society that it would be useless to look to it for help in a time of overwhelming peril.

Examination showed that the root cause of this situation was that psychology was using an inappropriate set of assumptions. Long before psychology came into existence it had been decided what it would find when it began its investigations. It was accepted that the new science of mind and behavior would find the same sort of mechanisms and mechanical interactions that the nineteenth century had found as it perfected the steam engine. This was not recognized for the fundamental method-ological error that it was: to decide in advance what your observations and experiments will find and then to do only, and regard only as valid, observations and experiments that fit your preconceptions. Thus psychology is the only field in which the findings were decided on before the field came into existence. It seems to be no coincidence that it is not prepared today to deal with its own central problems.

Since no meaningful or important aspects of human life fit the mechanical model, we more and more studied the unimportant aspects of human life that did. Our other solution to the problem was to abandon studying human beings (our primary subjects) as such for the study of entities that we could study in mechanical ways and with mechanical assumptions. These included rats and pigeons in the laboratory and, lately, computers. Experiments that we did on human beings were designed to demonstrate their mechanical and ratlike characteristics—and were successful. We then claimed that we had experimentally proven that human beings were essentially ratlike and machinelike in nature.

However, during this process, it became clear to the culture at large that if problems concerned the laboratory behavior of rats and pigeons, we *were* the experts to turn to. If, however, the problems were of the nature of how to stop killing each other, how to stop poisoning our planet, or how to stop our steadily increasing population growth, one had better turn elsewhere. Since this is a culture that sees science as the way to solve problems and the relevant science was clearly helpless to do so, an increasing pessimism and hopelessness has spread through all Western society.

Psychology chose one branch of the fork on the road to its becoming a science, which led to the present situation. As I have tried to show in this book, it was, considering the cultural orientation of the time, an inevitable choice.

Men and women of great dedication and sincerity made this choice in the deep belief that it would lead to a rich and productive path. It was in the hope of a better life for humanity that Wundt and Titchener tried to analyze consciousness into its smallest basic units, that Watson and Skinner tried to analyze behavior into reflexes and muscle twitchings, that thousands of other psychologists tried to understand human behavior through isolating one or another part of behavior or consciousness, being as objective as possible about their data, making metaphors of humankind and following their implications wherever they led, and, in general, determinedly pursuing the path of the most productive science of all times. They believed that this was the correct route and followed it with energy, devotion, and love.

It is always hard to see one's own assumptions and harder still to see that they are limited in scope or inapplicable in *this* situation. The assumptions that a science inevitably leads to quantification of your material, general laws covering all of your field, and precise prediction of the behavior of individual entities are so deeply ingrained in our thinking that they were almost unquestionable. Only very slowly have we begun to realize that they were inapplicable to a science of human consciousness and behavior.

Although it has taken us a long time to see the problem, it was described and investigated in detail at the end of the last century. It had started with Giambattista Vico's earlier studies of the field of history and the necessary methodology for it. Later Dilthey, Rickert, and Windelband generalized it to the social sciences in particular and psychology in particular. There were various names for the two scientific methods that gradually emerged as essential. Rénan called them "La Science de la Nature" and "La Science de la Humanité." Dilthey called them "Naturwissenschaft" and "Geisteswissenschaft." Windelband and later Gordon Allport called them "Nomothetic" and "Idiographic" science. Despite the different names, there was excellent agreement as to the structure and methods necessary for La Science de la Humanité—the science of human consciousness and behavior.

In three separate fields of the social sciences—ethology, history, and dynamic psychiatry—we see the new method being widely used. (It was also used with precision and excellence by good nursery school teachers!) Curiously, we find one specific individual close to the beginning of its use in all three.

Wilhelm Windelband was a friend of Freud. Lorenz described his influence on the new field of ethology. Collingwood wrote of his importance to its use in the field of history. Little known today, this important philosopher had an amazing effect on the social sciences.

Idiographic science, the science of human thought and behavior, does not have general laws. It does have a clear method. In it, one starts from the specific. I examine a person suffering from schizophrenia. I try to learn as much about him as I can, to comprehend him on as many levels as possible. I ask "Who is this person?" "Who is this schizophrenic?" "What is a schizophrenic?" "How does this schizophrenic differ from others I put in the same category?" I do not arrive at any laws carved in stone. I can never make exact predictions about the behavior of specific schizophrenics. But as I proceed, my understanding deepens. I learn more about what it is and feels like to be schizophrenic. The way to help people with this illness emerges. I can respond to them and know more what they see and how they perceive the world they are responding to. My "understanding" becomes a "standing under" the same sky and in the same world. It takes training, hard work, and a "disciplined subjectivity" to do this. It is as rigorous a scientific path as is that of La Science de la Nature.

This is how I would learn about painting and music. It is how I would learn about religious experience, heterosexual (or homosexual) love, grief over loss, creative expression, courage and steadfastness in the face of adversity, or any of the other important or meaningful parts of human life. And by "important" I mean as lived and defined by human beings, not as defined by a theoretical model. "Important" includes what we hold in common with the rest of the animal life on this planet— our needs to survive as individuals and as a species. It also includes what we have by virtue of being human: our psychological and spiritual needs, our needs to create beauty, our compassions, our fears and our aspirations, our hopes and fears, our ability to

> . . . *love thee to the depth and breadth and height*
> *My soul can reach, when feeling out of sight*
> *For the ends of Being and ideal grace . . .*
> *[To] love thee to the level of every day's*
> *Most quiet need by sun and candle-light.*

Our ability to work to design utopias for all and to build con-centration camps for many. Our Saint Teresas of Avila, our Beethovens, our Tamerlanes, and our Hitlers.

The laboratory and La Science de la Nature have a very real and important role to play in our attempt to learn about, to understand and comprehend, ourselves. The laboratory is an absolutely necessary place to test hypotheses and ideas arrived at through other means. As insights and comprehensions emerge, they must be put to proof in the laboratory, which thus becomes an integral and central part of our scientific endeavor to find out who we are and where we are going. Kept in its place, the experimental method and the laboratory are irre-placeable parts of our science; used wrongly, as they have often been in psychology, they spell disaster.

We are a complex and ever-developing species, full of joy and sadness, love and hate, selfishness and altruism, pettiness and grandeur. Complexity and change, however, have never been real blocks to scientific understanding and advancement. What does prevent the growth of a science is not using it properly: if the basic method we use is not related either to the data in the realm of experience we are studying or to the goals proper to that realm. Using and combining the two methods of science correctly can lead us into a deep and artistic, scientifically dis-ciplined comprehension of our comic and tragic species and can help psychology develop into a science that can help guide us out of the deadly traps we are in, a science that can enable us to avoid Armageddon. And, finally, on a more personal note:

At the age of nineteen, as a sophomore in college, I had discovered the still-young field of psychology. Out of a tumultuous childhood with frequent feelings of both failure and confusion, there was a sudden flash of recognition and hope. I had discovered what seemed like the ultimate adventure—a searching for what it meant to be human and in the human condition.

The path since then has been exciting and uneven. The struggle to find the most fruitful uses of this remarkable field of psychology brought peak experiences and ecstatic moments as well as periods of despair. For me, this struggle to sift the wheat from the chaff has brought both closure for the first phase of my life and great enthusiasm for the future. I hope that I have been able to share these feelings and the reasons for them in this book.

NOTES

Chapter 1: In a Dark Wood

1. M. R. Cohen, *Reason and Nature* (New York: Harcourt, Brace, 1931), p. 367.
2. K. Lewin, *Principles of Topological Psychology*, trans. F. and G. M. Heider (New York: McGraw-Hill, 1939), p. 13.
3. A. Toynbee, quoted in W. B. Walsh, *Perspectives and Patterns: Discourses on History* (Syracuse, N.Y.: University Press of Syracuse, 1962), p. 73.
4. *Psychological Monitor* 17, no. 6 (June 1981), p. 22.
5. Ibid., p. 24.

Chapter 2: Charting the Wrong Turn

1. S. Koch, "Psychology as Science," in S. F. Brown, *Philosophy of Psychology* (New York: Harper & Row, 1974), p. 6.
2. D. O. Hebb, "What Psychology Is About," *American Psychologist* 29 (1973), p. 74.

3. Koch, "Psychology as Science," p. 16.
4. A. Koestler, *The Ghost in the Machine* (New York: Random House, 1967), Appendix I.

Chapter 3: How to Train Specialists

1. A. Koestler, *The Ghost in the Machine* (New York: Random House, 1967), p. 15.
2. H. M. Prochansky, "For What Are We Training Our Graduate Students?" *American Psychologist* 27 (1972), p. 207.
3. J. Barzun, *A Stroll with William James* (New York: Harper & Row, 1983), p. 81.
4. L. Hudson, *The Cult of the Fact* (New York: Harper Torchbooks, 1973), pp. 40ff.

Chapter 4: The Laboratory and the World

1. N. Tinbergen, *The Animal in Its World* (Cambridge, Mass.: Harvard University Press, 1973), p. 10.
2. J. C. Flugel, *A Hundred Years of Psychology* (New York: Basic Books, 1964), p. 315.
3. J. Dewey, 1899 Presidential Address for American Psychological Association, in E. Hilgard, *American Psychology in Historical Perspective* (Washington, D.C.: American Psychological Association, 1978), p. 66.
4. Ibid., p. 75.
5. E. Fromm, *Psychology Today* (February 1986), p. 75.
6. A. N. Whitehead, *Science and the Modern World* (1926; reprint, New York: Mentor Books, 1948), p. 18.
7. D. Bannister, "Psychology as an Exercise in Paradox," *Bulletin of the British Psychological Society* 19 (1960), p. 24.
8. K. Popper, *The Poverty of Historicism* (1957; reprint, New York: Harper Torchbooks, 1964), p. 18.
9. D. G. Mook, "In Defense of External Validity," *American Psychologist* 38 (April 1983), p. 383.

10. See, for example, S. Sarason, *Psychology Misdirected* (New York: Free Press, 1981).
11. See, for example, W. Windelband, *Theories in Logic* (1912; reprint, New York: Philosophical Library, 1961); H. Rickert, *Science and History* (1912; reprint, New York: D. Van Nostrand, 1962); and R. G. Collingwood, *Essays in the Philosophy of History* (Austin: University of Texas Press, 1965).

Chapter 5: Numbers and Human Feelings

1. J. Bruner, *In Search of Mind* (New York: Harper & Row, 1983), p. 107.
2. H. Bergson, quoted in R. Haynes, *The Seeing Eye, the Seeing I* (London: Hutchinson, 1982), p. 63.
3. W. James, *The Principles of Psychology* (1890; reprint, New York: Dover, 1950), p. 230.
4. H. Bergson, Presidential Address, *Proceedings: Society for Psychological Research* 57 (1963) p. 159.
5. A. Koestler, quoted in J. Beloff, *New Directions in Parapsychology* (London: ELEK Science Press, 1974), p. 165.
6. K. Popper, *The Poverty of Historicism* (1957; reprint, New York: Harper Torchbooks, 1964), p. 3.
7. Ibid., p. viii.
8. I. Kant, *Critique of Pure Reason* (A-133), quoted in M. Polanyi, *Knowing and Being* (Chicago: University of Chicago Press, 1969), p. 105.
9. G. A. Miller, *Psychology: The Science of Mental Life* (New York: Harper & Row, 1962), pp. 322ff. See also G. Allport, "The Personalistic Psychology of William Stern," in B. J. Wolman, *Historical Roots of Contemporary Psychology* (New York: Harper & Row, 1968), pp. 321–37.
10. S. Sarason, *Psychology Misdirected* (New York: Free Press, 1981), p. 111.

Chapter 6: Making a Model of Man

1. A. Chapanis, "Men, Machines, and Models," in R. H. Mark, *Theories in Contemporary Psychology* (New York: Macmillan, 1966), p. 105.
2. *Advances* 2, no. 6 (1984), p. 4.
3. I. Berlin, "Notes on Alleged Relationism in 18th Century Thought," in L. Pompa and W. H. Dray, *Substance and Form in History* (Edinburgh: Edinburgh University Press, 1981), p. 13.
4. J. McK. Cattell, "Psychology as an Experimental Science," in E. Hilgard, *American Psychology in Historical Perspective* (Washington, D.C.: American Psychological Association, 1978), pp. 53ff.
5. G. Allport, "The Psychologist's Frame of Reference," *Psychological Bulletin* 37 (1940), pp. 14ff.
6. A. D. W. Malefist, *Images of Man* (New York: Knopf, 1974), p. 344.
7. A. Korzybski, Lecture to seminar, Lakeville, Connecticut, 1951.
8. F. A. Beach, "The Snark Was a Boojum," in T. E. McGill, ed., *Readings in Animal Behavior* (New York: Holt, Rinehart & Winston, 1965), pp. 3–15.
9. Ibid.
10. Ibid.
11. C. L. Kutscher, *Readings in Comparative Studies in Animal Behavior* (Waltham, Mass.: Xerox College Publishing, 1971), p. 2.
12. K. and M. Breland, "The Misbehavior of Organisms," *American Psychologist* (1961).
13. E. Cassirer, *The Myth of the State* (New Haven: Yale University Press, 1946), p. 6.
14. E. H. Madden, *Philosophical Problems of Psychology* (New York: Odyssey Press, 1962), p. 66.
15. M. C. Swabey, *The Judgement of History* (New York: Philosophical Library, 1954), p. 25.

Chapter 7: "God Is an Engineer"

1. J. B. Watson, personal communication to A. Jenness, 1932.
2. T. H. Huxley, "The Problematic Science: Psychology," in W. R. Woodward and M. G. Ash, eds., *Nineteenth-Century Thought* (New York: Praeger, 1988), p. 100.
3. R. E. Johnson, *In Quest of a New Psychology* (New York: Human Science Press, 1985), p. 16.
4. A. Toynbee, quoted in M. C. Swabey, *The Judgement of History* (New York: Philosophical Library, 1954), p. 95.
5. B. F. Skinner, *Science and Human Behavior* (New York: Macmillan, 1953), p. 169.
6. L. Kubie, K. Lashley, and D. O. Hebb, all quoted in M. Polanyi, *Knowing and Being* (Chicago: University of Chicago Press, 1969), p. 42.
7. Polyanyi, ibid.
8. G. Allport, "The Personalistic Psychology of William Stern," in B. J. Wolman, *Historical Roots of Contemporary Psychology* (New York: Harper & Row, 1968), p. 330.
9. R. M. Rilke, quoted in H. A. Hodges, *Wilhelm Dilthey* (New York: Oxford University Press, 1944), p. 25.
10. G. Santayana, *Reason in Science* (New York: Collier, 1962), p. 71.
11. L. Mumford, *Technics and Civilization* (New York: Harcourt, Brace, 1934), p. 76.
12. S. Koch, "Psychology as Science," in S. F. Brown, *Philosophy of Psychology* (New York: Harper & Row, 1974), p. 14.
13. A. S. Eddington, *The Nature of the Physical World* (New York: Macmillan, 1931), p. 467.
14. M. R. Cohen, quoted in D. A. Hollinger, *Morris Cohen and the Scientific Ideal* (Cambridge, Mass.: MIT Press, 1975), p. 99.
15. Paraphrased from R. G. Collingwood, "Human Nature and History," in P. Gardner, ed., *The Philosophy of History* (New York: Oxford University Press, 1974), p. 31.

16. S. Sarason, *Psychology Misdirected* (New York: Free Press, 1981), p. 10.
17. D. Berg and K. Smith, eds., *Exploring Clinical Methods for Social Research* (Palo Alto, Calif.: Sage Publications, 1985), p. 73.
18. Ibid.
19. C. Alderfer, quoted in ibid.
20. K. Lashley, quoted in Koch, "Psychology as Science," p. 19.
21. A. Angyal, *Foundations for a Science of Personality* (New York: The Commonwealth Fund, 1941), p. 24.
22. K. Goldstein, in H. Swaardemaker and C. Murchison, eds., *A History of Psychology in Autobiography* (New York: Russell & Russell, 1961), vol. 2, p. 154.
23. K. Lorenz, quoted in P. N. Lehner, *Handbook of Ethological Methods* (New York: Garland STPM Press, 1979), p. 11.
24. Collingwood, "Human Nature and History," p. 29.
25. G. Murphy, *Human Potentialities* (New York: Basic Books, 1958).
26. T. Szasz, "The Myth of Mental Illness," *American Psychologist* 15 (1960), p. 115.
27. G. Watson, "Moral Issues in Psychotherapy," *American Psychologist* 13 (1958), p. 575.
28. G. H. Turner, "Psychology—Becoming and Unbecoming," *Canadian Journal of Psychology* 14 (1960), pp. 153–56.
29. R. May, "Historical and Philosophical Presuppositions for Understanding Therapy," in O. H. Mowrer, ed., *Psychotherapy, Theory and Research* (New York: Ronald Press, 1953).

Chapter 8: Psychology and the Human Condition

1. S. Freud, quoted in L. LeShan and H. Margenau, *Einstein's Space and Van Gogh's Sky* (New York: Collier, 1982), p. 143.
2. N. Ackerman, *The Psychodynamics of Family Life* (New York: Basic Books, 1958).

3. C. Rogers, "Some Directions and End Points in Therapy," in O. H. Mowrer, ed., *Psychotherapy, Theory and Research* (New York: Ronald Press, 1953).

Chapter 9: Necessary Assumptions for a Human Science

1. F. A. Hayek, *The Counter-Revolution of Science* (Glencoe, Ill.: Free Press, 1952), p. 14.
2. L. Mumford, *Technics and Civilization* (1934; reprint, New York: Harcourt, Brace, 1963), p. 16.
3. R. G. Collingwood, "Human Nature and History," in P. Gardner, ed., *The Philosophy of History* (New York: Oxford University Press, 1974), p. 25.

Chapter 10: The Two Methods of Science

1. F. A. Hayek, *The Counter-Revolution of Science* (Glencoe, Ill.: Free Press, 1952), p. 15.
2. S. Freud, *An Analysis of a Case of Hysteria*, intro. Philip Rieff (1905; reprint, New York: Collier Books, 1963).
3. Rieff, ibid., p. 10.
4. Paraphrased from R. G. Collingwood, *Essays in the Philosophy of History* (Austin: University of Texas Press, 1965), p. xvi.
5. K. Lorenz, quoted in P. N. Lehner, *Handbook of Ethological Methods* (New York: Garland STPM Press, 1979), p. 172.
6. T. Roszak, *Why Astrology Endures* (San Francisco: Robert Briggs Associates, 1986), p. 1.

SELECTED BIBLIOGRAPHY
(and some sample viewpoints)

ALLPORT, G. W. "The Psychologist's Frame of Reference." *Psychological Bulletin* 37 (1940), pp. 72–78.

ANGYAL, A. *Foundations for a Science of Personality*. New York: The Commonwealth Fund, 1941.
". . . the essential difference is that the mechanical device is characterized by passivity, the organism by activity" (p. 37).

ARGYLE, M. *Social Interaction*. Chicago: Atherton Press, 1969.

BANNISTER, D. "Psychology as an Exercise in Paradox." *Bulletin of the British Psychological Society* 19 (1966), pp. 21–26.

BARZUN, J. *A Stroll with William James*. New York: Harper & Row, 1983.
"Whether we try to replace the mind by a computer or by an unconscious that does all the work, the result is the same. We have lost the individual and returned to the automaton whose study makes us more comfortable" (paraphrase of p. 47).

170

BEACH, F. A. "The Snark Was a Boojum." *Readings in Animal Behavior 1950.* Reprint. New York: Holt Rinehart & Winston, 1965.
"When the American comparative psychologist went hunting animal behavior, he found one animal—the albino rat, and it was a Boojum and the psychologist vanished softly and suddenly away" (paraphrase of p. 4).

BERLIN, I. *Historical Inevitability.* New York: Oxford University Press, 1954.

BERMAN, L. *The Religion Called Behaviorism.* New York: Boni & Liveright, 1927.
"Definitions always mutilate realities, and hence all dictionaries are the hospitals of ruptured and crippled ideas" (p. 11).

BRONOWSKI, J. *The Common Sense of Science.* Boston: Harvard University Press, 1978.

CHAPANIS, A. "Men, Machines and Models." *American Psychologist* 16 (1961), pp. 113–31.

CLAIBORNE, R. *God or Beast?* New York: W.W. Norton, 1974.
"Among the young psychologists whom [J. B.] Watson attracted to his banner, such words as 'unconsciousness,' 'sensation,' 'idea,' and 'pleasure' soon became as taboo as the word 'orgasm' at a Georgia Camp meeting" (p.23).

COHEN, M. R. *Reason and Nature.* New York: Harcourt Brace, 1937.
". . . the fields of psychology and sociology in which exercises in technical vocabulary frequently hide the paucity of substantial insight" (p. viii).

———. *Studies in Philosophy and History.* New York: Frederick Ungar, 1949.

COLLINGWOOD, R. G. *An Essay on Philosophical Method.* Oxford: Oxford University Press, 1933.

————. *Essays in the Philosophy of History.* Austin, Tex.: University of Texas Press, 1965.

————. "Human Nature and History." In P. Gardner, ed. *The Philosophy of History.* New York: Oxford University Press, 1974.
"A natural process is a process of events, a historical process is a process of thought" (p. 21).

COOLEY, C. H. *Selected Papers.* New York: Henry Holt, 1930.
"What should we think of a zoology which failed to give a life-like account of the animal?" (p. 332).
"The basis of reality for our knowledge of men is in sympathetic or dramatic perception; without these we are all in the air" (p. 333).

CROCE, B. *History: Its Theory and Practice.* Translated by D. Ainslie, Jr. New York: Russell & Russell, 1960.

DILTHEY, W. *Pattern and Meaning in History.* New York: Harper Torchbooks, 1961.

EYSENCK, H. J. *Sense and Nonsense in Psychology.* Baltimore Md.: Pelican, 1957.

FLUGEL, J. C. *A Hundred Years of Psychology.* New York: Basic Books, 1964.

GIORGI, A. *Psychology as a Human Science.* New York: Harper & Row, 1970.
"In the natural sciences we have knowledge and explanation, but in the human sciences we have understanding and interpretation" (p. 26).

GOLDSTEIN, K. In H. Zwaardemaker, and C. Murchison, eds. *A History of Psychology in Autobiography,* vol. C. New York: Russell & Russell, 1961.
"It is of the utmost importance that one evaluates any aspect of the organism in relation to the conditions of the organism as a whole. . . . The drive towards self-realization is not

merely a stimulus, but a driving force that puts the organism into action" (p. 150).

GUTHRIE, R. V. *Even the Rat Was White: A Historical View of Psychology.* New York: Harper & Row, 1976.

HAMMOND, K. R. *The Psychology of Egon Brunswik.* Holt, Rinehart & Winston, 1960.

HAYEK, F. A. *The Counter Revolution of Science.* Glencoe: Free Press, 1952.

———. *The Sensory Order.* Chicago: University of Chicago Press, 1952.
"It seems almost as though 'speculation' (which, be it remembered, is merely another word for thinking) has become so discredited among psychologists that it has to be done by outsiders who have no professional reputations to lose" (p. vi).

HAYES, C. J. H. *A Generation of Materialism.* New York: Haprer Torchbooks, 1960.

HILGARD, E. *American Psychology in Historical Perspective.* Washington, D.C.: N.P.A. Inc., 1978.

HINDE, R. A. *Ethology.* New York: Oxford University Press, 1982.

HODGES, H. A. *The Philosophy of Wilhelm Dilthey.* Westport, Conn.: Greenwood Press, 1974.

———. *Wilhelm Dilthey.* New York: Oxford University Press, 1946.
"We always understand more than we know" (p. 119).

HOLLINGER, B. A. *Morris R. Cohen and the Scientific Ideal.* Cambridge, Mass.: MIT Press, 1975.

HOLT, E. B. *The Freudian Wish.* New York: Holt & Co., 1915.
". . . coral reefs in the last analysis consist of positive and negative ions, but the biologist, geographer, or sea captain

would miss his point if he conceived of them in any such terms" (p. 160).

HUDSON, L. *The Cult of the Fact.* New York: Harper Torchbooks, 1942.

"There is no barrier between science and art. All arguments bearing on human life deserve to be heard within the same arena of debate. . . . Most social scientists who rely on . . . computers seem to abandon their powers of reasoning. . . . The research worker seems subtly to become the creature of the data–processing machinery, rather than vice-versa" (p. 12).

HUGHES, H. C. *Consciousness and Society.* 1961. Reprint. New York: Vintage/Random House, 1977.

"Under the influence of Social Darwinism 'heredity' and 'environment' replace conscious logical thought as the main determinants of human action" (p. 38). "[Pareto] squeezed the life blood out of human behavior until finally little more than a listing of hollow categories was left" (p. 224).

JOHNSON, R. C. *In Quest of a New Psychology.* New York: Human Sciences Press, 1935.

". . . cloister ourselves within the synthetic security of animal laboratories and normal distributions" (p. 16).

A very large number of academic studies in psychology have proven the obvious and well known with a tremendous amount of work and at great expense. A recent (1990) case in point was the Learning Environment Assessment Project, which examined more than two hundred children in twenty-two schools. It contrasted two groups of children. The first group had mothers who were pushier, more demanding, more critical, less affectionate, and had extremely high expectations. The second group had mothers who felt that "kids should be kids." The children in the first group tended to be less creative, have more test anxiety, and by the first grade, to have no academic advantages over the second.

This elaborate, careful, and expensive study showed what every early childhood educator and nursery school teacher has known for a long time. It reminds one of Ernst Cassirer's remark to William Stern about a similar research project: "One has to be a very educated psychologist to make a study of something so completely obvious."

KENDLER, H. H. *Psychology: A Science in Conflict.* New York: Oxford University Press, 1981.
"No one has suggested that patients should ask their psychotherapist for proof that his technique works. It is considered legitimate to ask a surgeon. . . . If you spent the same amount of money you do on psychotherapy on a trip, plastic surgery, a sailboat, would you get as good results? Why do we not know the answer to this?" (paraphrase of p. 353).

KIMBLE, G. A., AND CARMEZY, M. *Principles of General Psychology.* 2nd ed. New York: Ronald Press, 1963.
". . . psychology is a branch of natural science. [This is] . . . the most important idea you will get in your first course in psychology . . . human and animal behavior . . . can be described objectively, manipulated, controlled, and studied in the same way as other natural events" (p. 15).

KOCH, S. "Psychology as Science." In S. E. Brown, *Philosophy of Psychology.* New York: Harper & Row, 1974.

———. *A Study of a Science.* 6 vols. New York: McGraw-Hill, 1959–1963.

KOESTLER, A. *The Act of Creation.* 1940. Reprint. London: Pan Books, 1969.
"The word 'reflex,' as Sir Charles Sherrington has said, is a useful fiction" (p. 28).

———, AND SMYTHIES, J. R. *Beyond Reductionism.* Boston: Beacon Press, 1969.

———. *The Ghost in the Machine.* New York: Random House, 1967.

——. *Janus*. New York: Random House, 1978.

——. Letter, *The Humanist* (October 1951).
". . . nineteenth-century materialism—that of course is as dead as mutton. What will come after I do not know. We live in an earthquake and the new pattern of things has not yet crystallised."

KOHL, L. *The Age of Complexity*. New York: Mentor, 1965.

KUTSCHER, C. L. *Readings in Comparative Studies in Animal Behavior*. Waltham, Mass.: College Publications, 1971.

LEWIN, K. *Principles of Topological Psychology*. Translated by Fritz Heider and Grace M. Heider. New York: McGraw-Hill, 1936.

LOCKARD, R. B. "The Albino Rat! A Defensible Choice or a Bad Habit." *American Psychologist* 23 (1968), pp. 734–42.
". . . we would be astonished if astronomers studied only earth and applied false generalizations to the rest of the universe" (p. 741).

LORENZ, K. quoted in Lehner, P. N. *Handbook of Ethological Methods*. New York: Garland STPM Press, 1979.
"The current belief that only quantitative procedures are scientific . . . is a fallacy, dictated by the 'technomorphic' thought habits acquired in our culture when dealing preponderantly with inorganic material" (p. 15).

MCDOUGALL, W. *Outline of Psychology*. New York: Charles Scribner & Sons, 1923.
"The two principal alternative routes are (1) that of mechanical science, which interprets all its processes as mechanical cause and effect, and (2) that of the science of mind, for which purposive striving is a fundamental category" (p. 39).

MACKRIEL, R. A. *Dilthey! Philosopher of the Human Studies*. Princeton, N.J.: Princeton University Press, 1975.

MILLER, G. A. *Psychology: The Science of Mental Life*. New York: Harper & Row, 1962.

". . . there is a long list of creditable sciences that do not rely on measurement. . . . In truth a good case could be made that if your knowledge is meager and unsatisfactory, the last thing in the world you should do is make measurements. . . . One can still find psychologists making extravagantly elaborate measurements just to demonstrate how scientific a psychologist can be" (p. 79). "A rat is not especially typical of anything but rats" (p. 229).

MOOK, D. A. "In Defense of External Validity." *American Psychologist* 38 (1983), pp. 379–87.

MUMFORD, L. *Technics and Civilization*. 1934. Reprint. New York: Harcourt Brace, 1963.
"Like the Englishman in France who believed that bread was the right name for le pain, each culture believes that every other kind of space and time is a perversion of the real space and time in which it lives" (p. 18).

MUNROE, R. *Schools of Psychoanalytic Thought*. New York: Dryden Press, 1955.

MURPHY, C. *Historic Introduction to Modern Psychology*. New York: Harcourt Brace, 1949.

MURPHY, G., AND KOVACH, J. K. *Historical Introduction to Modern Psychology*. 2d ed. New York: Harcourt Brace Jovanovich, 1972.
"However important the nomothetic aspects must be for certain purposes of science, there are realities viewed through the idiographic telescope which cannot be ignored" (p. 415).

POLANYI, M. *Knowing and Being*. Chicago: University of Chicago Press, 1969.
"All true scientific research starts with hitting on a deep and promising problem, and this is one-half of the discovery" (p. 118).

———. "Logic and Psychology." *American Psychologist* 23 (1968), pp. 27–43.

POPPER, K. A. *The Poverty of Historicism*. New York: Harper Torchbooks, 1957.

PROSHANSKY, H. M. "For What Are We Training Our Graduate Students?" *American Psychologist* 27 (1972), pp. 205–12.

RICKERT, H. *Science and History*. 1912. Reprint. New York: D. Van Nostrand, 1962.
"There are sciences which do not aim at the discovery of natural laws or even at the formation of general concepts. They do not want to produce 'ready-made' clothes that fit Paul just as well as they do Peter; they propose to represent reality which is never general, but always individual, in its individuality. . . . In regard to what is general, the historian will agree with Goethe. We will make use of it, but we do not cherish it. We cherish only the individual" (p. 55).

RUESCH, J., AND BALESA, A. *Communication: The Social Matrix of Psychiatry*. New York: Norton, 1968.
"The foundations of psychoanalysis were laid in the same scientific period as the theories of classical economics and both reflect the physics of the 1850s" (p. 247).

RUSSELL, B. *Human Knowledge: Its Scope and Limits*. New York: Simon & Schuster, 1948.

SANTAYANA, G. *Reason in Science*. New York: Collier Books, 1962
"Physics cannot account for the minute motion and pulsation in the earth's crew of which human affairs are a portion. Human affairs have to be surveyed under categories lying closer to those employed in memory and legend" (p. 57).
——*Winds of Doctrine*. 1912. Reprint. New York: Harper Torchbooks, 1957.
"Man is certainly an animal that, when he lives at all, lives for ideals" (p. 6).

SARASON, S. P. *Psychology Misdirected*. New York: Fell Press, 1981.

"Psychology as a science and practice were married. Let us bypass the possibility that these are grounds for annulment because they never really slept together. (Each member of the marriage has accused the other of impotence, deceit and other of man's less endearing attributes, sexual and otherwise)" (p. 34).
"The concept of 'intelligence' is a social invention, inevitably reflecting time and place, not a 'thing' in an individual" (p. 111).

SCHILPP, P. A., ed. *Albert Einstein, Philosopher Scientist.* Vol. 1. New York: Harper Torchbooks, 1957.

SILVERMAN, I., ed. *Generalizing from Laboratory to Life.* San Francisco: Jossey-Bass, 1981.

SPERRY, R. W. "Psychology's Mentalist Paradigm and the Religion/Science Tension." *American Psychologist* 41 (August 1988), pp. 607–20.

SWABEY, M. C. *The Judgment of History.* New York: Philosophical Library, 1954
"Consciousness carries this authority within itself, and those who re-create the past must reach beyond the public records to more intimate acquaintance" (p. 56).

TINBERGEN, N. *The Animal in Its World.* Cambridge, Mass.: Harvard University Press, 1973.

TOLMAN, E. C. *Purposive Behavior in Animals and Men.* 1932. Reprint. Appleton-Century-Crofts, 1967.

——, and Brunswik, E. "The Organism and the Causal Texture of the Environment." *Psychological Review* 42 (1935), pp. 43–47.

——, quoted in Bruner, J. *In Search of Mind.* New York: Harper & Row, 1983.
"Behavior reeks with purpose" (p. 109).

TYRELL, G. N. A. *The Nature of Human Personality*. London: G. Allen and Unwin, 1934.
"The fact that some lines of science are marked out and selected, while others are passed over and ignored is in itself significant. In fact a good deal of light could be thrown on psychology by studying the unconscious behavior of the mind by the psychologist" (p. 60).

VAN OVER, R. *Psychology and ESP*. New York: Mentor, 1972.

VICO, G. *The New Science*. Translated by T. A Bergin and M. H. Fisch. 1744. Reprint. Ithaca, N.Y.: Cornell University Press, 1984.

———. *On the Study of Methods of our Time*. Translated by E. Gianturco. 1709. Reprint. New York: Bobbs-Merrill, 1965.

WATSON, J. B. *Behavior: An Introduction to Classical Psychology*. New York: Holt & Co., 1914.
"In passing from the unicellular organisms to man, no new principle is needed" (p. 318).

WHITEHEAD, A. N. *Science and the Modern World*. New York: Mentor, 1948.

WINDELBAND, W., quoted in Plantigna, K. *Historical Understanding in the Thought of Wilhelm Dilthey*. Toronto: University of Toronto Press, 1980.
"Nomothetic sciences are sciences of laws, idiographic sciences are sciences of events. The first teaches what always is, the second what once was" (p. 25).

———. *Theories in Logic*. 1912. Reprint. New York: Philosphical Library, 1961.

WOLMAN, B. J. *Historical Roots of Contemporary Psychology*. New York: Harper & Row, 1968.
"The time may come when psychologists will be less afraid than they are now to delve into problems of personal emo-

tion (lest they seem emotional) or into the study of senti-
ments (lest they appear sentimental) or into the riddles of
personhood (lest they become personal)" (p. 337).

WOODWARD, R. E., AND ASH, M. G. *The Problematic Science: Psychology in Nineteenth-Century Thought.* New York: Praeger
Publishers, 1982.

INDEX

Note: Alphabetization letter-by-letter, mac as mc. An *n* following a page number indicates that the entry is found in a footnote on that page.